JEREMIAH
BIBLE STUDY SERIES

1 & 2 TIMOTHY & TITUS

THE WAY TO LIVE AND LEAD FOR CHRIST

DR. DAVID JEREMIAH

Prepared by Peachtree Publishing Services

HarperChristian
Resources

1 & 2 Timothy & Titus
Jeremiah Bible Study Series
© 2020 by Dr. David Jeremiah

Requests for information should be addressed to:
HarperChristian Resources, 3900 Sparks Dr. SE, Grand Rapids, Michigan 49546

ISBN 978-0-310-09176-9 (softcover)
ISBN 978-0-310-09177-6 (ebook)

All Scripture quotations are taken from The Holy Bible, New King James Version®. © 1982 by Thomas Nelson. Used by permission. All rights reserved.

Any internet addresses (websites, blogs, etc.) and telephone numbers in this study guide are offered as a resource. They are not intended in any way to be or imply an endorsement by HarperChristian Resources, nor does HarperChristian Resources vouch for the content of these sites and numbers for the life of this study guide.

HarperChristian Resources titles may be purchased in bulk for church, business, fundraising, or ministry use. For information, please e-mail ResourceSpecialist@ChurchSource.com.

Produced with assistance of Peachtree Publishing Service (www.PeachtreePublishingServices. com). Project staff include Christopher D. Hudson, Randy Southern, and Peter Blankenship.

23 24 25 26 27 LBC 7 6 5 4 3 Printed in the United States of America

CONTENTS

INTRODUCTION TO
The Letters of 1 & 2 Timothy and Titus

"If you instruct the brethren in these things, you will be a good minister of Jesus Christ, nourished in the words of faith and of the good doctrine which you have carefully followed. But reject profane and old wives' fables, and exercise yourself toward godliness. For bodily exercise profits a little, but godliness is profitable for all things" (1 Timothy 4:6–8). History tells us the apostle Paul was a remarkable individual who worked tirelessly to spread the gospel. When we read accounts of his life, such as the one told in Acts, we might think he accomplished these feats on his own. But the truth is that Paul had a team that helped him. His mission was to spread the gospel as far and wide as he could, so he was rarely in one place for any extended period of time. Yet the congregations he founded needed shepherding. For this reason, he recruited godly men such as Timothy and Titus to minister in his absence. Paul knew the task would not be easy. He knew they would face many challenges. So he sent them letters—such as the ones we have in our Bible—to instruct, encourage, and equip them in this role.

1 TIMOTHY

Author and Date

The writer of this letter identifies himself as "Paul, an apostle of Jesus Christ" (1:1). Early church fathers such as Polycarp (AD 59–156), Clement of Rome (AD 35–99), and Justin Martyr (AD 100–165) each made allusions to 1 & 2 Timothy and Titus (collectively known as the "pastoral letters"), and

Irenaeus (writing around AD 180) noted they were penned by Paul. Although the letters do not contain themes typically found in Paul's letters, and the vocabulary and style do not necessarily match his other letters, the personal details he includes about Timothy align with what we know about Paul's life from Acts. It is likely Paul composed the letter c. AD 62, after being released from arrest in Rome (see Acts 28), when he was again allowed to travel.

Background and Setting

Paul helped found the church in Ephesus during his second missionary journey (see Acts 18:18–21) and ministered there for three years during his third missionary journey (see 19:1–41). Following his release from prison in Rome, sometime after the events depicted in Acts, he returned to the city with Timothy, whom he considered his "son in the faith" (1 Timothy 1:2). Paul eventually journeyed on to regions in Macedonia, but he left Timothy behind to minister in the church and confront certain false teachers who had infiltrated the congregation. Paul wrote this first letter from Macedonia to Timothy to instruct, inspire, and encourage him in this task.

Key Themes

Several key themes are prominent in 1 Timothy. The first is that *believers in Christ must possess sound doctrine and practices in worship* (see 1 Timothy 1–2). The city of Ephesus had been a center of pagan worship for centuries and was famous for its temple dedicated to the Greek goddess Artemis. As such, the city presented a unique challenge for believers in knowing how to lead a righteous life in the midst of a pagan culture. Paul thus offers instructions to Timothy on how to pray, worship, and maintain sound doctrine in the midst of competing influences.

A second theme is that *believers in Christ must be instructed by godly leaders* (see 1 Timothy 3). Paul emphasizes the importance of entrusting ministry to those who are pursuing godliness and encourages Timothy to surround himself with fellow laborers whose lives consistently reflect the influence of Christ. Paul assists him in his search by giving him a list of qualities and character traits to look for in prospective candidates.

A third theme is that *believers in Christ must avoid false teaching and be good servants in God's kingdom* (see 1 Timothy 4–6). Paul was particularly concerned in advising Timothy on how to recognize false teachers in the church and not allow them to gain a foothold among the members. He instructed Timothy to encourage believers to flee from such teachings, pursue godly qualities (such as love, patience, and gentleness), and look for ways to serve the body of Christ. He urged Timothy to always fight for righteousness, be faithful to God's Word, and remember that believers in Christ are recognized by the way they live.

2 TIMOTHY

Author and Date

The writer of this letter also identifies himself as "Paul, an apostle of Jesus Christ" (1:1). Once again, though the vocabulary and style do not match his other letters (most likely in this case due to the personal nature of the letter), the details the writer includes align with what we know about Paul's life. It is likely Paul wrote the letter two to three years after penning 1 Timothy and shortly before his death in AD 67 at the hands of Emperor Nero. This was evidently the final letter that Paul wrote (see 2 Timothy 1:8, 16; 4:6–13) and was penned from a Roman prison.

Background and Setting

Paul had written in his first letter that he hoped to visit Timothy soon in Ephesus (see 1 Timothy 3:14–15). It is unknown whether this visit ever took place, but it clear that by the time Paul wrote his second letter, he was no longer in Macedonia but imprisoned in Rome, "suffer[ing] trouble as an evildoer, even to the point of chains" (2 Timothy 2:9). The Roman Emperor Nero's persecution of Christians had intensified, and Paul recognized that his ministry on this earth was coming to an end. He would soon be martyred for his faith—"Poured out as a drink offering" (4:6). So Paul wrote to ask Timothy to join him in Rome (see 4:9, 21).

Key Themes

Several key themes are prominent in this letter. The first is that *believers in Christ must remain faithful to the Lord in spite of what they are facing* (see 2 Timothy 1). Paul reminds Timothy that suffering is just part of the normal Christian life, and believers are called to persevere in their faith regardless of their present circumstances. As they do this, they can identify with Christ Himself, who suffered and endured faithfully on their behalf.

A second theme is that *believers in Christ must continue to pursue truth and sound doctrine* (see 2 Timothy 2–3). Paul frequently refers to "the truth" that Timothy has been given and charges him to guard this treasure that has been entrusted to him. As he does this, he will be able to recognize any false doctrines or teachings that threaten to infiltrate the church. He urges believers to leave behind their self-centered lives and stand firm in God's grace and truth. In doing this, they will be recognized as Jesus' disciples.

A third theme is that *believers need to stay focused on the mission* (see 2 Timothy 4:1–8). Paul concludes his letter with a challenge for us to stay focused on our calling of sharing the gospel. We are to convince, rebuke, exhort, and endure in our mission and avoid fruitless arguments that take us away from this goal. Paul's focus was ever on the prize that was awaiting him in heaven, and he wanted to bring as many people into God's kingdom as he could. This should be the ultimate goal of our lives as well.

TITUS

Author and Date

The writer of this letter identifies himself as "Paul, a bondservant of God and an apostle of Jesus Christ" (1:1). As with the other pastoral letters, the vocabulary and style are not typical of what is found in Paul's other letters, but the details he includes align with what we know about Paul's life and his relationship with Titus. It is likely Paul composed the letter c. AD 63–64, sometime after visiting the church on the isle of Crete and leaving Titus in charge there.

Background and Setting

Little is known about Titus. Luke never mentions him in the book of Acts, and while he appears to have not been as close to Paul as Timothy, he was still a trusted associate. Paul writes in his letter to the Galatians that Titus was a Gentile, and the fact that he was not circumcised after converting to Christ played a key role in Paul securing the right to a law-free gospel for Gentiles (see Galatians 2:1, 3). Paul entrusted Titus with the tasks of delivering a letter to the church at Corinth (see 2 Corinthians 2:3–4, 13; 7:6–16) and gathering the Corinthian gift for the poor of Jerusalem (see 8:16–24). Paul evidently travelled with Titus to Crete sometime between AD 64–63, and he left Titus there to provide leadership to the new church (see Titus 1:5).

KEY THEMES

Several key themes are prominent in this letter. The first theme is that *believers in Christ must have sound doctrine to live in godliness* (see Titus 1:1–4; 2:1). Paul states in his opening greeting to Titus that he is an apostle "according to the faith of God's elect and the acknowledgment of the truth which accords with godliness" (verse 1). He then encourages Titus to "speak the things which are proper for sound doctrine" (2:1) so the congregation can grow in godliness.

A second theme is that *believers in Christ need virtuous leaders* (see Titus 1:5–16; 2:2–10). Paul carefully defines the qualities and virtues that elders in the church should possess. He also describes behaviors that elders should avoid—primarily in regard to their speech. As Paul notes, there were many "idle talkers and deceivers" present in the congregation (1:10), and Titus was to make sure these individuals were not in a position to influence others.

The third theme is that *believers in Christ should be trained by God's grace and live in obedience to Him* (see Titus 2:11–3:11). Paul instructs Titus to remind the believers in Crete that they were saved "not by works of righteousness" but "according to [God's] mercy" and have now become His "heirs according to the hope of eternal life" (3:5, 7). At the same time, Paul urges, that "those who have believed in God should be careful to maintain good works" (verse 8).

Key Applications

The letters that Paul wrote to Timothy and Titus give us an in-depth look at pastoral ministry in the church. In many ways, they serve as a blueprint for the qualities and character traits that are needed for anyone who desired to serve in church ministry. As we read the letters, we should keep in mind that Paul wrote them to two actual pastors to address actual issues in their churches and provide them with sound solutions that still apply in our times. As Paul's greetings insist, those pastors did not face their struggles alone, and neither do we today. As we study these letters, we can be assured—like Timothy and Titus—of God's grace, mercy, and peace.

FIGHT THE GOOD FIGHT

1 Timothy 1:1–20

GETTING STARTED

What are some causes in your life that are important to you? Why are those causes important?

SETTING THE STAGE

In Acts, we read that Paul travelled to the city of Lystra, located in Asia Minor, during his first missionary journey (see 14:8–18). At this time, it is likely Paul met Timothy and led him and his family to faith in Christ. Luke tells us Timothy's father was Greek and his mother was Jewish (see 16:1)—a situation that probably caused him to be treated as an outsider by the greater Jewish community. Regardless, Timothy had dedicated himself to the study of Jewish Scripture since he was a child (see 2 Timothy 3:15).

When the time came for Paul to begin his second missionary journey, he again travelled to Lystra and asked Timothy to accompany him and Silas on their venture. Before setting out, Timothy agreed to be circumcised in order to remove potential barriers to his ministry among the Jews (see Acts 16:1–3). Timothy helped evangelize Philippi and Thessalonica (see Philippians 2:19–24; 1 Thessalonians 3:1–10). When Paul and Silas left Thessalonica, Timothy stayed behind to help guide and influence the fledgling church. He then moved on to Corinth (see 1 Corinthians 4:16–17; 16:10–11), where he acted as Paul's liaison to the church. From there, he went to Ephesus, where he prepared the churches in the region for Paul's visit.

Timothy was one of the few people who remained faithful to Paul after his imprisonment. Following Paul's release from prison in Rome (which occurred sometime after the events depicted in Acts), Timothy again travelled with Paul to Ephesus. Paul continued on into Macedonia, but he left Timothy behind in Ephesus to serve as pastor to the growing congregation that was in need of spiritual leadership.

At some point in Paul's journey, he pauses to write a personal letter to Timothy to encourage him in his new role and make sure he is ready for the task. As we find in this opening section, he begins by reminding Timothy of his responsibilities—first, as a discerner of, and protector against, false teachings; and second, as a fighter for God-honoring causes. Paul's advice resonates with anyone who has ever stepped into a position of leadership and authority: remember your calling, cling to your faith, and fight the good fight for Christ.

EXPLORING THE TEXT

Greeting (1 Timothy 1:1–7)

---

¹ Paul, an apostle of Jesus Christ, by the commandment of God our Savior and the Lord Jesus Christ, our hope,

² To Timothy, a true son in the faith:

Grace, mercy, and peace from God our Father and Jesus Christ our Lord.

³ As I urged you when I went into Macedonia—remain in Ephesus that you may charge some that they teach no other doctrine, ⁴ nor give heed to fables and endless genealogies, which cause disputes rather than godly edification which is in faith. ⁵ Now the purpose of the commandment is love from a pure heart, from a good conscience, and from sincere faith, ⁶ from which some, having strayed, have turned aside to idle talk, ⁷ desiring to be teachers of the law, understanding neither what they say nor the things which they affirm.

---

1. Paul opens the letter by stating he is an "an apostle of Jesus Christ," which is his customary way of establishing his identity to his readers. How does Paul go on to identify Timothy (see verse 2)? How would this designation authenticate Timothy as his successor in the church?

2. What characteristics of godliness does Paul say must be present in the teaching of God's Word? What should be avoided when teaching God's Word (see verses 5–6)?

No Other Doctrine (1 Timothy 1:8–11)

[8] But we know that the law is good if one uses it lawfully, [9] knowing this: that the law is not made for a righteous person, but for the lawless and insubordinate, for the ungodly and for sinners, for the unholy and profane, for murderers of fathers and murderers of mothers, for manslayers, [10] for fornicators, for sodomites, for kidnappers, for liars, for perjurers, and if there is any other thing that is contrary to sound doctrine, [11] according to the glorious gospel of the blessed God which was committed to my trust.

---

3. Paul quickly moves into the main concern that had motivated him to write the letter: the presence of false teachers in the church. Evidently, some of these teachers were using the law of Moses to bolster and support their false claims. For whom does Paul say the law was made? What does the law reveal about a person (see verses 8–10)?

----

4. Paul knew that no one (aside from Christ) has ever followed the law perfectly, and thus it has no power to save us from sin. What had God revealed to Paul instead (see verse 11)?

_____

_____

_____

_____

_____

_____

_____

_____

_____

_____

_____

Glory to God for His Grace (1 Timothy 1:12–16)

12 And I thank Christ Jesus our Lord who has enabled me, because He counted me faithful, putting me into the ministry, 13 although I was formerly a blasphemer, a persecutor, and an insolent man; but I obtained mercy because I did it ignorantly in unbelief. 14 And the grace of our Lord was exceedingly abundant, with faith and love which are in Christ Jesus. 15 This is a faithful saying and worthy of all acceptance, that Christ Jesus came into the world to save sinners, of whom I am chief. 16 However, for this reason I obtained mercy, that in me first Jesus Christ might show all longsuffering, as a pattern to those who are going to believe on Him for everlasting life.

5. Paul now makes a short digression to remind Timothy of his own life and how God has used him in spite of his past. How does Paul say that his life before finding Christ differs from his life at the time when he wrote this letter? How did the change make him uniquely qualified to talk about God's abundant grace to others (see verses 12–15)?

_____

_____

_____

_____

_____

_____

_____

6. Paul had been a former persecutor of the church and considered himself a "chief" among sinners. What did Jesus demonstrate in extending mercy to Paul (see verses 15–16)?

_____

_____

_____

_____

_____

_____

Fight the Good Fight (1 Timothy 1:17–20)

[17] Now to the King eternal, immortal, invisible, to God who alone is wise, be honor and glory forever and ever. Amen.

[18] This charge I commit to you, son Timothy, according to the prophecies previously made concerning you, that by them you may wage the good warfare, [19] having faith and a good conscience, which some having rejected, concerning the faith have suffered shipwreck, [20] of whom are Hymenaeus and Alexander, whom I delivered to Satan that they may learn not to blaspheme.

7. Paul concludes this section with a brief prayer (or *doxology*), in which he praises the unmatched character of God. Why do you think Paul includes this prayer after reflecting on his own life? What is his personal charge to Timothy (see verses 17–18)?

_____

_____

_____

_____

_____

8. Paul names two false teachers (Hymenaeus and Alexander) and states they have been "delivered to Satan," which likely refers to their removal from the church. What had these men rejected? What did Paul want these men to learn (see verses 19–20)?

_____

_____

_____

_____

_____

_____

REVIEWING THE STORY

Paul sets the tone of his letter by referring to Timothy as his "true son in the faith" (1:2), and like a concerned father, he wants to make sure Timothy is fully equipped to handle the situation. False teachers had infiltrated the church in Ephesus. Among other things, these teachers were urging the believers to place themselves under Jewish law. Paul reminds Timothy that the power of the law pales in comparison to the power of the gospel of Christ. He urges Timothy to stay strong and remember that he is not alone in the fight.

9. From a personal and spiritual standpoint, how did Paul view Timothy (see 1 Timothy 1:2)?

10. What was the primary purpose of the Old Testament law (see 1 Timothy 1:9–10)?

11. What did Paul want Timothy to know about the direction his own life had taken since his encounter with the risen Christ (see 1 Timothy 1:12)?

12. What phrase does Paul use to suggest that people had been expecting big things from Timothy for some time (see 1 Timothy 1:18)?

_____

_____

_____

_____

_____

_____

APPLYING THE MESSAGE

13. What difference does it make in your life to know that Jesus extended mercy to Paul, the "chief" among sinners? What does this tell you about God's grace?

_____

_____

_____

_____

_____

_____

_____

14. Who are some individuals you have mentored and encouraged in the faith? How have they helped you?

_____

_____

_____

_____

_____

_____

REFLECTING ON THE MEANING

As Paul concludes the opening section of his first letter to Timothy, he gives his protégé a solemn responsibility to "wage the good warfare" (1:18). Jesus is clear that the same responsibility belongs to all His followers. As he said to His disciples, "Blessed are you when they revile and persecute you, and say all kinds of evil against you falsely for My sake. Rejoice and be exceedingly glad, for great is your reward in heaven, for so they persecuted the prophets who were before you" (Matthew 5:11–12). If we live for Jesus, we will face attacks just as He did.

So, how do we "wage the good warfare" when these attacks come into our lives? Paul offers some clues in his instructions to Timothy. First, *we fight the good fight with faith*. As believers, we allow the Holy Spirit to guide us into battle. If He prompts us to engage with someone, we must listen to His instruction and act. We may not feel prepared or comfortable, but we must trust God to give us the wisdom, courage, patience, and authority we need.

Second, *we fight the good fight with a clear conscience*. We can never lose sight of the fact that we always represent Christ in this world. Given this, we must resist the urge to "fight dirty" by engaging in personal attacks or broad generalizations, twisting or misrepresenting God's words to "win a point," or letting our anger or frustration get the best of us.

Third, *we fight the good fight for the benefit of others*. As Paul instructs Timothy in the art of battle, he mentions two people who failed to fight the good fight: Hymenaeus and Alexander. Paul's ultimate goal is that the men "may learn not to blaspheme" (1 Timothy 1:20). He wants them to be restored. He has their best interests at heart.

Paul fights the good fight because he is genuinely concerned about others. He knows from his own story as a former persecutor of the church that no one is too far gone to receive God's incredible gift of grace. He had found salvation and purpose in his relationship with Christ. This same attitude and loving concern should drive every one of our pointed encounters with others.

JOURNALING YOUR RESPONSE

What does it mean to "fight the good fight" when it comes to your faith in Christ?

A WITNESS TO THE WORLD

1 Timothy 2:1–15

GETTING STARTED

What are some practices you employ to live at peace with others?

_____

_____

_____

_____

_____

_____

_____

_____

_____

_____

_____

SETTING THE STAGE

There are several passages in Scripture that deal with the roles of men and women in the church. One of these is found in this next section of Paul's letter, where we read, "Let a woman learn in silence with all submission . . .

I do not permit a woman to teach or to have authority over a man, but to be in silence. For Adam was formed first, then Eve" (1 Timothy 2:11–13). Many people today are uncomfortable with this statement, but we need to keep a few points in mind as we read Paul's words.

First, it is significant that Paul first addresses the men in the church before he speaks about the women. Paul viewed men as leaders in the home—and some of them as leaders in the church. The issue at stake is how they were to pray: "lifting up holy hands" (verse 8). They were to worship God out of a sincere heart and a life marked by holiness. They were also to do this "without wrath and doubting," which were signs of an improper attitude in worship.

Paul has this instruction in mind when he then addresses the women, stating "in like manner also," they are to worship God from a sincere heart. In this regard, there is evidence that particular adornments of the time—such as "braided hair or gold or pearls or costly clothing" (verse 9)—were considered marks of sinful motives. It was not that all outward adornments were considered wrong. Paul simply wanted the women in the church to avoid all appearances of worldly portrayals of ostentation and seduction.

It is also important to understand that in the first century, Jewish women were not allowed to study the Scriptures or worship with men. However, in spite of that norm, Paul states that he wants the women to worship and learn right alongside the men. Yet he desires for this to be done "decently and in order" (1 Corinthians 14:40), with the women being taught when the entire church gathered together. There is evidence the false teachers in Ephesus were encouraging women to flaunt their freedom in Christ and act disruptively.

What we find in Paul's instruction is thus based on the pattern established in Scripture. It is evident from the first marriage recorded—Adam and Eve—that God ordained a certain order in the husband-wife relationship. This order established the husband as leader in the first marriage and in all marriages that followed. Paul states that this order also has implications for church leadership. The gender norms for eldership must follow the norms for marriage.

EXPLORING THE TEXT

Pray for All Men (1 Timothy 2:1–4)

¹ Therefore I exhort first of all that supplications, prayers, intercessions, and giving of thanks be made for all men, ² for kings and all who are in authority, that we may lead a quiet and peaceable life in all godliness and reverence. ³ For this is good and acceptable in the sight of God our Savior, ⁴ who desires all men to be saved and to come to the knowledge of the truth.

1. Based on Paul's words in his other letters, we know he often prayed for close friends and relatives. However, whom does he instruct believers to pray for in this passage? What is the ultimate goal of their praying for everyone and respecting authority (see verses 1–2)?

_____

_____

_____

_____

2. Paul says that living a quiet and peaceable life is good and acceptable to God. Why do you think living in such a way reflects well on Christ? What is God's desire for all people (see verses 3–4)?

_____

_____

_____

_____

_____

One God and One Mediator (1 Timothy 2:5–8)

> [5] For there is one God and one Mediator between God and men, the Man Christ Jesus, [6] who gave Himself a ransom for all, to be testified in due time, [7] for which I was appointed a preacher and an apostle—I am speaking the truth in Christ and not lying—a teacher of the Gentiles in faith and truth.
>
> [8] I desire therefore that the men pray everywhere, lifting up holy hands, without wrath and doubting . . .

3. Paul stresses that just as there is only *one* God, there is only "one Mediator between God and men." Why is Jesus the only one who can fill the role of Mediator (see verses 5–6)?

_____

_____

_____

_____

_____

_____

4. Paul was concerned with the removal of any barriers to the Christian community uniting in effective prayer. How does Paul say believers can truly be united in prayer (see verse 8)?

_____

_____

_____

_____

_____

_____

_____

Women in the Church (1 Timothy 2:9–11)

⁹ . . . in like manner also, that the women adorn themselves in modest apparel, with propriety and moderation, not with braided hair or gold or pearls or costly clothing, ¹⁰ but, which is proper for women professing godliness, with good works. ¹¹ Let a woman learn in silence with all submission.

5. Paul calls on men and women to reject the world's standards of measuring worth and beauty and instead adopt heaven's standard. What was the standard that Paul called on the women of Ephesus to achieve (see verses 9–11)?

_____

_____

_____

_____

_____

_____

6. Paul's use of the term *silence* as it pertains to women in the church likely refers back to his instruction for all believers to lead "a quiet and peaceable life" (2:2). Why would this be important given Paul's emphasis on the church being a model to the outside world? What were the dangers of the outside world witnessing an unruly gathering of believers?

_____

_____

_____

_____

_____

Assurance for Women (1 Timothy 2:12–15)

> [12] And I do not permit a woman to teach or to have authority over a man, but to be in silence. [13] For Adam was formed first, then Eve. [14] And Adam was not deceived, but the woman being deceived, fell into transgression. [15] Nevertheless she will be saved in childbearing if they continue in faith, love, and holiness, with self-control.

7. Scholars believe Paul's instructions for women not to teach or have authority over men applied to public gatherings of believers (see verse 8). In the highly patriarchal world of Paul's day, such a situation could have caused those in the outside world to criticize the church. Why would this have run contrary to everything Paul was trying to achieve?

_____

_____

_____

_____

_____

8. Paul assures women that the pain of childbirth is not to be understood as a sign of God's displeasure. Rather, God's salvation is promised to all—including those who contribute to God's creation through childbearing. What does Paul say that women (and men) must persist in doing to assure they will be saved (see verse 15)?

_____

_____

_____

_____

_____

REVIEWING THE STORY

Paul emphasizes to Timothy that the call to prayer is also a call to think about God and His work in humanity. He encourages believers to pray for everyone—including those in authority. Paul then reminds Timothy that Jesus is able to serve as a Mediator between believers and God because He gave Himself as a sacrifice in their place. Paul then stresses the particular roles of men and women in public gatherings that he expects his churches to follow. Above all, the church must look to Christ and not conform to the stereotypes of the world. Furthermore, believers must demonstrate the healing and freedom enacted by the good news of Jesus' work.

9. What docs praying for those in authority have to do with people being saved and coming to know the truth (see 1 Timothy 2:1–4)?

10. How did Paul instruct men and women to behave in the church (see 1 Timothy 2:8–10)?

11. What specific instructions did Paul give to the women in the church in Ephesus when it came to modesty in public gatherings (see 1 Timothy 2:9)?

_____

_____

_____

_____

_____

12. What instructions did Paul give to women in the church when it came to teaching in public gatherings (see 1 Timothy 2:11–12)?

_____

_____

_____

_____

_____

APPLYING THE MESSAGE

13. What are some ways that you are seeking to lead a quiet and peaceable life?

_____

_____

_____

_____

_____

14. What are some ways you can show honor and respect to those in authority over you?

_____

_____

_____

_____

_____

REFLECTING ON THE MEANING

Paul ends this much-debated passage in 1 Timothy with an explanation about Adam and Eve. As you read his words, it is important to remember his basic point is to state that women—like men—should be allowed to learn and study as disciples of Jesus. He asks Timothy to consider what happened when Eve was deceived. The events of the Fall show that women, just like men, can be deceived and need to learn and grow. Both Adam's and Eve's sin were *deliberate*. They knew what they were doing and both *chose* to sin.

Perhaps one of the most puzzling parts of this passage is the mention of childbearing. Paul's words here should not be interpreted as though he sees childbearing as a form of divine punishment. In fact, he offers encouragement and assurance to women that even though childbearing is difficult and painful—possibly the most trying moment of a woman's life—it is not to be understood as a curse. God has promised salvation to *all*—women and men alike—who follow Jesus in "faith, love, and holiness, with self-control" (1 Timothy 2:15).

Remember that Paul wrote these instructions to build up the church—both men and women—and provide sound teaching on how to live in such a way that outsiders would be attracted to Christ. Like Paul, we must think wisely and pray diligently about our witness to the world. We are called not to conform to the practices of a secular world, but rather be transformed in our hearts and minds through the gospel. We are then to transform the world around us as we walk and work in step with what the Holy Spirit is doing.

JOURNALING YOUR RESPONSE

Are there some ways in which your life has conformed to the patterns of the world? If so, how will you seek God's power in those areas so they can be transformed into His image?

TRAITS OF A GODLY LEADER

1 Timothy 3:1–16

GETTING STARTED

What do you think are the three most important qualities for a church leader to possess?

_____

_____

_____

_____

_____

_____

_____

_____

_____

_____

_____

_____

_____

_____

_____

_____

SETTING THE STAGE

One of the apostle Paul's most pressing concerns when it came to the church in Ephesus was that its leaders adhered to practices for godly living. Paul had already hinted about two members that had strayed (see 1 Timothy 1:20), and he wanted Timothy to choose the right people to lead the church in the right way. It was vital to Paul that those in leadership not only *preached* the gospel but also *lived* the gospel in the way they conducted all of their affairs.

Paul thus begins this section by urging Timothy to choose those who desired to be bishops and deacons in the church based on certain qualities and character traits. In this context, *bishops* were those who had oversight over the entire church, while *deacons* carried out practical church functions in leadership and serving roles. Bishops had to be spiritually mature and completely devoted disciples of Christ. Likewise, deacons had to be God-honoring individuals with servants' hearts who were growing in spiritual maturity.

By setting the bar high, Paul was helping Timothy minimize leadership problems that could occur down the line. While no person can maintain God's perfect standards all the time—and all of us need His forgiveness at times—leaders in the church have to be more spiritually mature because they have great influence on the spiritually immature. As James stated, "My brethren, let not many of you become teachers, knowing that we shall receive a stricter judgment" (3:1). Paul had seen many teachers fall into error and lead unsuspecting believers astray. He needed to prevent this by making sure leaders not only "talked the talk" but "walked the walk."

The qualifications that Paul lists go beyond the immediate circumstances of Timothy and the church in the city of Ephesus. So, as you work your way through this passage, ask yourself how these qualifications and requirements can be applied to church leadership candidates today. And also ask yourself how *you* are living up to these standards that Paul outlines.

EXPLORING THE TEXT

Qualifications of Overseers (1 Timothy 3:1–4)

> ¹This is a faithful saying: If a man desires the position of a bishop, he desires a good work. ²A bishop then must be blameless, the husband of one wife, temperate, sober-minded, of good behavior, hospitable, able to teach; ³not given to wine, not violent, not greedy for money, but gentle, not quarrelsome, not covetous; ⁴one who rules his own house well, having his children in submission with all reverence.

1. Paul makes it clear there is nothing wrong with a person aspiring to hold the position of bishop. This is actually a noble pursuit. However, in what seven positive qualities does the person seeking this position need to be mature (see verse 2)?

_____

_____

_____

_____

_____

2. Paul next adds five negative qualities that aspiring leaders are to avoid—many of which were found in the false teachers in the church (see 1 Timothy 6:4–5, 9–10). What are those five qualities that those seeking Christian maturity must avoid (see verse 3)?

_____

_____

_____

_____

A Good Testimony (1 Timothy 3:5–7)

⁵ (For if a man does not know how to rule his own house, how will he take care of the church of God?); ⁶ not a novice, lest being puffed up with pride he fall into the same condemnation as the devil. ⁷ Moreover he must have a good testimony among those who are outside, lest he fall into reproach and the snare of the devil.

3. The word *novice* in this passage derives from the Greek word for "newly planted." What is the risk of placing a novice in an important leadership role (see verse 6)?

_____

_____

_____

_____

_____

_____

4. In addition to spiritual maturity and healthy relationships, it was essential that prospective leaders had a "good testimony," or good reputation, with those outside the church. Given Paul's overarching mission to the Gentiles, why was it so important for a bishop to have a good reputation among people outside the church (see verse 7)?

_____

_____

_____

_____

_____

Qualifications of Deacons (1 Timothy 3:8–12)

8 Likewise deacons must be reverent, not double-tongued, not given to much wine, not greedy for money, 9 holding the mystery of the faith with a pure conscience. 10 But let these also first be tested; then let them serve as deacons, being found blameless. 11 Likewise, their wives must be reverent, not slanderers, temperate, faithful in all things. 12 Let deacons be the husbands of one wife, ruling their children and their own houses well.

5. Paul now provides positive and negative qualifications for deacons. What is the one positive quality that deacons must possess? What three negative qualities are they to avoid (see verse 8)? How do these compare to the qualifications for bishops listed in verses 2–4?

_____

_____

_____

_____

_____

_____

6. The Greek word translated "their wives" seems to imply these women were also serving in ministry in some capacity. What qualifications does Paul say they must have (see verse 11)?

_____

_____

_____

_____

_____

_____

The Great Mystery (1 Timothy 3:13–16)

¹³ For those who have served well as deacons obtain for themselves a good standing and great boldness in the faith which is in Christ Jesus.

¹⁴ These things I write to you, though I hope to come to you shortly; ¹⁵ but if I am delayed, I write so that you may know how you ought to conduct yourself in the house of God, which is the church of the living God, the pillar and ground of the truth. ¹⁶ And without controversy great is the mystery of godliness:

> God was manifested in the flesh,
> Justified in the Spirit,
> Seen by angels,
> Preached among the Gentiles,
> Believed on in the world,
> Received up in glory.

---

7. Paul's words in verse 15 might be better translated as, "Conduct yourself in a way that befits a member of God's family." Paul wanted to ensure the family of believers in Ephesus—in "God's house"—knew how to conduct themselves in this way. How does Paul describe this "house" to add force and solemnity to his directives (see verse 15)?

_____

_____

_____

_____

_____

_____

_____

_____

_____

8. In the religions of Paul's day, the idea of a *mystery* was something most people didn't understand. The few who did understand often intentionally kept the rest in the dark. But the Christian mystery has been revealed to *all*. What is that mystery (see verse 16)?

REVIEWING THE STORY

Paul offers essential qualifications for the offices of bishop and deacon. Most of these qualifications did not align with the cultural norms of his day. This was intentional, for Paul wanted to stress to Timothy that the Christian life does *not* align with the norms of secular society but with the truth of the "mystery of godliness" (see verse 16), which is Christ. The church is to be the stabilizing force of God's truth and grace in the world. It must share in community life, grounded in the mystery of Christ, and thereby serve as a witness to the world. After all, what the world knows of God will be based on the life and witness of His people.

9. Why do you think it is important for a bishop to be "blameless" (see 1 Timothy 3:2)?

----

10. What might cause a bishop to fall into reproach (see 1 Timothy 3:7)?

11. What kind of home life did Paul want deacons to have (see 1 Timothy 3:12)?

12. What urgency did Paul feel in writing these instructions (see 1 Timothy 3:14–15)?

APPLYING THE MESSAGE

13. How do you respond to the idea that the qualifications Paul sets forth for bishops and deacons are standards to which all Christians should aspire?

_____

_____

_____

_____

_____

_____

_____

_____

_____

14. How are you seeking to live your life according to these qualifications?

_____

_____

_____

_____

_____

_____

_____

_____

_____

_____

_____

REFLECTING ON THE MEANING

In this section of Paul's letter, he lays out qualifications that leaders of God's family must possess. These qualities relate not only to the words a leader speaks but also to the actions such a leader performs. So, how can you become this kind of leader—the kind who sets an example for those in the body of Christ and those still outside? I believe there are six key traits that you must incorporate into your life to be this kind of leader in the church.

First, you must show up. If you want to set an example and make a difference in your congregation, you have to show up for church. You have to get involved and invest yourself in the lives of others.

Second, you must prove yourself faithful. You must speak the truth in love in your personal interactions. You do what you say you are going to do. You offer a listening ear to those who need it then keep private what is entrusted to you. You stay above the fray where backbiting or gossip is concerned.

Third, you keep your lines of communication static-free. You resolve conflict before it gets a foothold. You apologize quickly and sincerely when you're in the wrong. You confront others in a caring way when you've been wronged.

Fourth, you are accountable to others. In order to function well as a leader in the church, you must first function well as a spouse and a parent in the home. You need your family members to help you maintain your balance and let you know when they feel neglected or sense your priorities are starting to shift. Your team should also include fellow leaders—people who understand the challenges of leadership.

Fifth, you become a disciple who makes disciples. You encourage and nurture God's calling in others. You ask God to work in their lives through the prompting of His Holy Spirit.

Sixth, you prioritize your own spiritual growth. This includes practices of regular prayer, Bible study, and quiet time spent listening to God. You ask the Holy Spirit to give you valuable perspective and wisdom you can use in your leadership role. As you incorporate these traits into your life, you will reflect well on "the house of God, which is the church of the living God, the pillar and ground of the truth" (1 Timothy 3:15).

Journaling Your Response

Which of these qualities do you need to work to better develop in your life? What practical steps will you take to grow in these areas?

A SPIRITUAL WORKOUT

1 Timothy 4:1–16

GETTING STARTED

What are some ways that you care for your physical, your emotional, and your spiritual health?

_____

_____

_____

_____

_____

_____

_____

_____

_____

_____

_____

_____

_____

_____

_____

_____

_____

_____

SETTING THE STAGE

Those called to leadership in the church tend to view their main task as often thinking of others and seldom thinking of themselves. They recognize that Jesus called His followers to "go therefore and make disciples of all the nations" (Matthew 28:19) and to "wash one another's feet" in service (John 13:14). But this attitude often leads to burnout. Far too many leaders today have experienced the horrible reality of physical and emotional exhaustion, family problems, fear of losing their job, and concerns that while they should be setting an example of godly living for the church, their inner turmoil makes them feel they are doing the opposite.

Paul puts the spotlight on this issue in this next section of his letter and provides clear, powerful, and wise advice on the need to care for our spiritual lives. He instructs Timothy to "give attention to reading, to exhortation, to doctrine" (1 Timothy 4:13), to "not neglect the gift" that is in him " (verse 14), and to "take heed to [himself] and to the doctrine" (verse 16). Each of these instructions is crucial for leaders today, yet they are often set aside and forgotten when such leaders find themselves under pressure.

Paul knows that Timothy is facing formidable opponents in Ephesus—false teachers such as Hymenaeus and Alexander. These men already had ensnared several believers in their bogus philosophy. They had likely presented themselves as educated authorities and experts in all things religious. Paul wants to make sure that Timothy doesn't fall for their routine or yield to their "expertise." So he exposes the false teachers for who and what they are.

But Paul also reminds Timothy of who *he* is—a disciple of Jesus who is capable of turning the tide against the false teachers in the Ephesian church through the power of the Holy Spirit. He actually instructs Timothy to *embrace* his youth and set an example for believers young and old, just as he had set an example for Timothy. Most of all, Paul reminds Timothy to hold fast to his training and to emphasize Christian doctrine in his teachings. He gives Timothy the responsibility to steer the Ephesian church in the right direction until he can get there.

EXPLORING THE TEXT

The Great Apostasy (1 Timothy 4:1–5)

¹ Now the Spirit expressly says that in latter times some will depart from the faith, giving heed to deceiving spirits and doctrines of demons, ² speaking lies in hypocrisy, having their own conscience seared with a hot iron, ³ forbidding to marry, and commanding to abstain from foods which God created to be received with thanksgiving by those who believe and know the truth. ⁴ For every creature of God is good, and nothing is to be refused if it is received with thanksgiving; ⁵ for it is sanctified by the word of God and prayer.

1. Paul was frustrated that some members of the Ephesian church had "departed from the faith" and were being led astray by false teachers. What were some of the teachings that were causing the believers in Ephesus to depart from the faith (see verses 1–3)?

2. In Paul's day, a false teaching known as *dualism* was circulating in the church that claimed the physical body was all evil but the spirit was all good, alive, and well. How does Paul respond to this false teaching in these verses (see verses 4–5)?

_____

_____

_____

_____

_____

_____

A Good Servant of Jesus Christ (1 Timothy 4:6–8)

⁶ If you instruct the brethren in these things, you will be a good minister of Jesus Christ, nourished in the words of faith and of the good doctrine which you have carefully followed. ⁷ But reject profane and old wives' fables, and exercise yourself toward godliness. ⁸ For bodily exercise profits a little, but godliness is profitable for all things, having promise of the life that now is and of that which is to come.

3. Paul desires Timothy to "be a good minister of Jesus Christ." What does Paul say is necessary for him to do so he can effectively teach others (see verse 6)?

_____

_____

_____

_____

_____

_____

4. In the time of the apostle Paul, athletic facilities known as *gymnasia* were central to the community life of Hellenistic cities. Ephesus, and most of the other cities Paul visited on his journeys, were thoroughly Hellenized. Paul does not disparage physical training in this passage, but how does he say it compares to godliness (see verses 7–8)?

_____

_____

_____

_____

_____

Trust the Living God (1 Timothy 4:9–12)

⁹ This is a faithful saying and worthy of all acceptance. ¹⁰ For to this end we both labor and suffer reproach, because we trust in the living God, who is the Savior of all men, especially of those who believe. ¹¹ These things command and teach.

¹² Let no one despise your youth, but be an example to the believers in word, in conduct, in love, in spirit, in faith, in purity.

5. Paul notes the saying he has quoted—"Godliness is profitable for all things, having promise of the life that now is and of that which is to come" (verse 8)—is truthful and worthy of acceptance. What had Paul endured to lead people to godliness (see verse 10)?

_____

_____

_____

_____

_____

6. Timothy may have been in his late thirties when Paul wrote this letter to him, which was still considered young for a teacher in first-century Jewish culture. What did Paul say about this to Timothy? In what areas did he want Timothy to be an example to the believers in Ephesus as a way of overcoming the "liability" of his age (see verse 12)?

_____

_____

_____

_____

_____

_____

Take Heed to Your Ministry (1 Timothy 4:13–16)

13 Till I come, give attention to reading, to exhortation, to doctrine. 14 Do not neglect the gift that is in you, which was given to you by prophecy with the laying on of the hands of the eldership. 15 Meditate on these things; give yourself entirely to them, that your progress may be evident to all. 16 Take heed to yourself and to the doctrine. Continue in them, for in doing this you will save both yourself and those who hear you.

7. In Paul's day most people were illiterate, so a common practice was to have the letters read out loud in front of the congregation. Why do you think the reading of Scripture was at the top of Paul's to-do list for Timothy (see verse 13)?

_____

_____

_____

_____

_____

8. Paul was concerned for Timothy's continued growth—not only for his protégé's own sake, but also for the sake of those he was leading. For this purpose, in what ways does Paul exhort Timothy to exercise his gifts and look to his own spiritual health (see verses 14–16)?

_____

_____

_____

_____

_____

REVIEWING THE STORY

Paul opens this next section of his letter by returning to the topic of false teachers in the church. He points out the heresy these teachers were proclaiming—which involved forbidding people to marry and eating only certain foods—was a preview of things to come during the end times. Paul emphasizes that believers should be grateful for _all_ of God's creation and that "nothing is to be refused if it is received with thanksgiving" (verse 4). Paul then instructs Timothy on the importance of exercising godliness— purposefully focusing on reading God's Word, exhorting others to follow Christ, and studying godly doctrine. Paul tells his younger coworker in the faith that "spiritual workouts" will benefit Timothy as well as the people he has been called to lead.

9. What should our attitude be toward the things God has given us to enjoy (see 1 Timothy 4:3)?

_____

_____

_____

_____

10. How does Paul refer to the false teachings that Timothy was dealing with in Ephesus (see 1 Timothy 4:7)?

_____

_____

_____

_____

_____

_____

11. How did Paul instruct Timothy to deal with the potentially awkward situation of leading a congregation of people who were older than him (see 1 Timothy 4:12)?

_____

_____

_____

_____

_____

_____

12. How did the leaders of the early church affirm their support of Timothy before he left for Ephesus (see 1 Timothy 4:14)?

_____

_____

_____

_____

_____

_____

APPLYING THE MESSAGE

13. Which of Paul's instructions in this section are easy for you to follow? Which are more difficult? Explain.

_____

_____

_____

_____

_____

_____

_____

_____

_____

_____

_____

_____

14. In what areas do you need spiritual training in order to grow as a disciple of Jesus and be an example to others?

_____

_____

_____

_____

_____

_____

_____

_____

_____

_____

_____

_____

REFLECTING ON THE MEANING

Paul provides instruction to Timothy in this section that is equally valuable for Christians today. He tells Timothy—and us—to first look to our own growth in godliness so we can then effectively nurture others in their growth. As we "give attention," "give [ourselves] entirely," and "take heed" (verses 13, 15–16) of the sound doctrine we have received, we will grow in spiritual maturity and ready ourselves to fully engage in serving God.

There are three questions we can ask ourselves as we seek to actively move "toward godliness" (verse 7). First, *are we prepared to grow in our relationship with God?* Paul writes in Philippians, "Not that I have already attained, or that I'm already perfected; but I press on, that I may lay hold of that for which Christ Jesus has laid hold of me" (3:12). These seem like the words of someone just starting out in ministry, but in reality, the apostle wrote them at the *close* of his ministry. After years of service, Paul was still maturing in his relationship with God.

Second, *are we prepared to meet the resistance of our spiritual adversary?* Spiritually mature Christians will attest to the fact that whenever God urges them to do something new in their spiritual lives, the devil unleashes his fiercest attacks. Our enemy is a master of distraction and will do everything he can to get our minds on something other than exercising godliness.

Third, *are we prepared to replace distractions with that which is most important?* We live in a day of confused priorities and self-destructive behaviors that we employ to fill the void of unmet needs in our lives. We feel we just *have* to do this and *have* to do that in order to be happy . . . and we quickly become distracted. Instead, Paul says that we should put these distractions aside and focus on exercising ourselves toward godliness (see 1 Timothy 4:7).

As we do this, we will discover the truth that the apostle Paul discovered: "For bodily exercise profits a little, but godliness is profitable for all things, having promise of the life that now is and of that which is to come" (verse 8).

JOURNALING YOUR RESPONSE

Which of these three questions hits closest to home in your life? Why?

HONOR IN THE CHURCH
1 Timothy 5:1–25

GETTING STARTED

What are some ways your church cares for the health and wellbeing of its members?

_____

_____

_____

_____

_____

_____

_____

_____

_____

_____

_____

_____

_____

_____

SETTING THE STAGE

In this next section of Paul's letter, we get a sense of the complexity of Timothy's job. In a broad sense, Timothy was the leader of the church in

Ephesus. But in a narrower sense, he was the leader of a group of older men, a group of older women, a group of younger men, and a group of younger women. He was also in charge of church leaders and churchgoers.

Each group had a unique perspective on the church, brought a unique set of needs, presented a unique set of challenges, and required a unique approach and sensitivity. There was no one-size-fits-all leadership model in Ephesus—nor were there any ministry "specialists" as we have today. Timothy's staff didn't include a young adult pastor or a children's minister. Paul, Timothy, and other church leaders were still trying to figure out what Christian ministry looked like in a foundational church setting.

Paul obviously empathizes with the challenges Timothy faces. But the apostle is adamant in his instructions . . . particularly as they relate to widows and elders. Paul is concerned, not about the expense of caring for widows, but rather that those who receive support will become idle and complacent in their responsibilities. Paul also wants to be certain that elders are honored, as their leadership was essential to the survival and success of the church. This included ensuring that elders leading the church were compensated.

As we know from Paul's other letters, he personally chose not to accept support from the churches where he was currently ministering. But he did not intend for others to follow this example. Rather, he makes it clear that the ministry these elders provided was essential—and they should therefore have the right to be paid for their good work.

EXPLORING THE TEXT

Treatment of Church Members (1 Timothy 5:1–7)

¹ Do not rebuke an older man, but exhort him as a father, younger men as brothers, ² older women as mothers, younger women as sisters, with all purity.

³ Honor widows who are really widows. ⁴ But if any widow has children or grandchildren, let them first learn to show piety at home

and to repay their parents; for this is good and acceptable before God. [5] Now she who is really a widow, and left alone, trusts in God and continues in supplications and prayers night and day. [6] But she who lives in pleasure is dead while she lives. [7] And these things command, that they may be blameless.

---

1. Underlying Paul's advice to Timothy on ministering to various groups in the church is the model of the church as "the house of God" (see 1 Timothy 3:15). What guidelines does Paul give Timothy for engaging with each demographic of this "family" (see verses 1–2)?

_____

_____

_____

_____

_____

2. Widows presented a challenge for the church. At the time, wives rarely inherited anything when their husbands died, and many had to rely on others for care, support, and survival. How does Paul recommend that Christians rise to this challenge (see verses 3–7)?

_____

_____

_____

_____

_____

_____

Honor True Widows (1 Timothy 5:8–12)

---

[8] But if anyone does not provide for his own, and especially for those of his household, he has denied the faith and is worse than an unbeliever.

⁹ Do not let a widow under sixty years old be taken into the number, and not unless she has been the wife of one man, ¹⁰ well reported for good works: if she has brought up children, if she has lodged strangers, if she has washed the saints' feet, if she has relieved the afflicted, if she has diligently followed every good work.

¹¹ But refuse the younger widows; for when they have begun to grow wanton against Christ, they desire to marry, ¹² having condemnation because they have cast off their first faith.

---

3. Most of the people in Paul's day recognized their obligation to care for their loved ones. They provided for the widows in their families out of a sense of responsibility and fairness. Why was it essential for believers to do the same (see verse 8)?

_____

_____

_____

_____

_____

_____

4. In Roman society, women under the age of sixty were considered capable of remarrying and capable of working. Why does Paul set this age limit—and establish the other requirements in the passage—for the church's support of widows (see verses 9–12)?

_____

_____

_____

_____

_____

_____

Honor the Elders (1 Timothy 5:13–18)

¹³ And besides they learn to be idle, wandering about from house to house, and not only idle but also gossips and busybodies, saying things which they ought not. ¹⁴ Therefore I desire that the younger widows marry, bear children, manage the house, give no opportunity to the adversary to speak reproachfully. ¹⁵ For some have already turned aside after Satan. ¹⁶ If any believing man or woman has widows, let them relieve them, and do not let the church be burdened, that it may relieve those who are really widows.

¹⁷ Let the elders who rule well be counted worthy of double honor, especially those who labor in the word and doctrine. ¹⁸ For the Scripture says, "You shall not muzzle an ox while it treads out the grain," and, "The laborer is worthy of his wages."

5. Apparently some of the younger widows in Ephesus, who were being fully supported by the church, were being "idle" and had fallen into gossiping and stirring up trouble. What did Paul want them to do instead? How would this benefit those widows who were in dire need and could not support themselves (see verses 13–15)?

6. While many translations use the term "double honor" to describe what Paul states the elders are owed, the Greek term more naturally refers to money rather than respect. What is Paul thus teaching in regard to compensating pastors for their work (see verses 17–18)?

_____

_____

_____

_____

_____

_____

_____

Observe These Things (1 Timothy 5:19–25)

¹⁹ Do not receive an accusation against an elder except from two or three witnesses. ²⁰ Those who are sinning rebuke in the presence of all, that the rest also may fear.

²¹ I charge you before God and the Lord Jesus Christ and the elect angels that you observe these things without prejudice, doing nothing with partiality. ²² Do not lay hands on anyone hastily, nor share in other people's sins; keep yourself pure.

²³ No longer drink only water, but use a little wine for your stomach's sake and your frequent infirmities.

²⁴ Some men's sins are clearly evident, preceding them to judgment, but those of some men follow later. ²⁵ Likewise, the good works of some are clearly evident, and those that are otherwise cannot be hidden.

7. Paul's instruction for dealing with accusations against an elder from multiple witnesses conforms to the Old Testament tradition (see Deuteronomy 19:15) and the teachings of Jesus (see Matthew 18:16).

Why does Paul recommend that Timothy deal with the private sins of elders in a public forum (see verses 19–20)?

_____

_____

_____

_____

_____

8. Paul knew that those in leadership roles were not immune to sin, including the sins of pride, arrogance, and sexual immorality. Paul thus instructed Timothy to not appoint someone to a church leadership position prematurely. How did Paul expect Timothy himself to behave in his role as a pastor of the church (see verses 21–25)?

_____

_____

_____

_____

_____

REVIEWING THE STORY

In this section of Paul's letter, he offers Timothy practical leadership tips on how to deal with various groups in the congregation. He begins by setting forth certain guidelines that widows must meet in order to qualify for support from the church. Paul does this not to minimize church expenditures but to maximize the women's ability to care for themselves. Paul then emphasizes the necessity of giving elders their due as well as the importance of holding elders accountable when they betray the trust given to them. The central concern behind all of Paul's instructions to Timothy is about how to properly live together as the family of God.

9. Where does the primary responsibility for caring for widows lie (see 1 Timothy 5:4)?

_____

_____

_____

_____

_____

_____

_____

10. What criteria did Paul set for widows to qualify for church support (see 1 Timothy 5:9–10)?

_____

_____

_____

_____

_____

_____

_____

_____

11. What scenario was Paul trying to avoid in advising Timothy not to support young widows in the church (see 1 Timothy 5:13–15)?

_____

_____

_____

_____

_____

_____

12. Why was it important for Timothy to remain impartial
(see 1 Timothy 5:21–22)?

_____

_____

_____

_____

_____

APPLYING THE MESSAGE

13. What is your responsibility as a member of the body of Christ to
widows and those who cannot support themselves?

_____

_____

_____

_____

_____

_____

14. What is your responsibility to elders and other leaders in the church?

_____

_____

_____

_____

_____

_____

_____

REFLECTING ON THE MEANING

Paul was deeply concerned about the church caring for its members. For him, it was related to his most central theological concern—that the church, in Jesus Christ and by the power of the Spirit, was the renewed family of God. The church's "family life" must thus reflect that reality.

Even in this age of specialized ministry, elders in the church—pastors and church leaders—still have a responsibility to work with different groups in the congregation and thereby maintain the health of God's family. The challenges of that task are as daunting and rewarding today as they were 2,000 years ago. As members of our local church congregation, we all have a responsibility to support our leaders in their tasks.

I believe there are five key ways that we can do this. First, *we can pray for wisdom, discernment, insight, and patience for our leaders*. We must understand that our leaders are human, under constant pressure, and often stretched beyond what they feel they can handle. The more we understand and appreciate the nuances of church leadership, and put ourselves into "their shoes," the better equipped we will be to offer them our support.

Second, *we can offer sincere encouragement, gratitude, and appreciation for the work our elders perform* . We can show patience and understanding when they fall short. We can intervene when we hear grumbling or complaints from others about church leaders.

Third, *we can act as ambassadors or representatives of our groups at church*. This involves getting involved in our community and acquainting ourselves with our church family's struggles. We can then meet with church leaders to discuss ways to address those needs.

Fourth, *we can seek to solve certain problems ourselves*. As we work with others, we can lessen the workload of elders by meeting specific needs— such as caring for "widows" and others under financial and emotional stress—in our church by ourselves. In the process, we will strengthen the spirit of community and the bond of fellowship within our group.

Fifth, *we can reach across the aisle*. We can bridge the distance between various groups that are represented in the church. We can create a spirit of oneness in our congregation that will allow our leaders to more effectively and efficiently do the jobs they are called to do.

JOURNALING YOUR RESPONSE

How can you better support the leaders in your own church community?

_____

_____

_____

_____

_____

_____

_____

_____

_____

_____

_____

_____

_____

_____

_____

_____

_____

_____

_____

_____

_____

_____

_____

_____

_____

_____

GODLINESS AND CONTENTMENT

1 Timothy 6:1–21

GETTING STARTED

How would you define *contentment*?

_____

_____

_____

_____

_____

_____

_____

_____

_____

_____

_____

_____

_____

_____

_____

_____

_____

Setting the Stage

Paul concludes his first letter to Timothy with a timeless charge for believers to recognize they are called to lived transformed lives for Christ. Furthermore, the family of God is called to model this different way of living to the outside world. Paul calls Timothy and the believers in Ephesus to have the courage to do so. This same call from Paul extends to us today.

This final section can certainly be seen as an indictment against modern Western society, in which people are absorbed by the relentless pursuit of wealth. Our society often views money as the highest and greatest good. People trip over one another in their pursuit of riches and financial security. They bring about their own ruin by their greed.

Ironically, all of this is done in the name of *contentment*. The old saying that "money can't buy happiness" is given lip service today, but not much else. In fact, most of the messages we receive from the world are that if we just had a little bit more money . . . *then* we would be truly happy. Life soon becomes the pursuit of happiness regardless of the cost to anyone else. We feel it is a basic human right. But in reality, it is a basic human wrong.

Paul tackles these misguided pursuits head-on. He provides specific details to Timothy on how to organize the church into a healthy community where God's grace is worked out and brings contentment to all its members. He gives instruction on pursuing worthwhile virtues that will actually lead to contentment and makes it clear that genuine faith in God, our good Creator, leads us in an entirely different direction than our self-centered pursuits.

Exploring the Text

Honor Masters (1 Timothy 6:1–5)

> [1] Let as many bondservants as are under the yoke count their own masters worthy of all honor, so that the name of God and His doctrine may not be blasphemed. [2] And those who have believing masters, let

them not despise them because they are brethren, but rather serve them because those who are benefited are believers and beloved. Teach and exhort these things.

[3] If anyone teaches otherwise and does not consent to wholesome words, even the words of our Lord Jesus Christ, and to the doctrine which accords with godliness, [4] he is proud, knowing nothing, but is obsessed with disputes and arguments over words, from which come envy, strife, reviling, evil suspicions, [5] useless wranglings of men of corrupt minds and destitute of the truth, who suppose that godliness is a means of gain. From such withdraw yourself.

---

1. Bondservants, or slaves, made up a large portion of the population of Ephesus—and thus of the Ephesian church. What unique opportunity does Paul say that bondservants have in their relationships with their masters (see verses 1–2)?

_____

_____

_____

_____

_____

2. In the opening of this letter, Timothy was commanded to "teach no other doctrine" than the one he had received from the apostle Paul (1:3). What happens in the family of God when these particular guidelines are not followed (see verses 3–5)?

_____

_____

_____

_____

_____

_____

Error and Greed (1 Timothy 6:6–10)

⁶ Now godliness with contentment is great gain. ⁷ For we brought nothing into this world, and it is certain we can carry nothing out. ⁸ And having food and clothing, with these we shall be content. ⁹ But those who desire to be rich fall into temptation and a snare, and into many foolish and harmful lusts which drown men in destruction and perdition. ¹⁰ For the love of money is a root of all kinds of evil, for which some have strayed from the faith in their greediness, and pierced themselves through with many sorrows.

3. Paul asserts that the true sign of *godliness* is *contentment*. What does he consider necessary to achieve this state of contentment? (see verses 6–8)?

_____

_____

_____

_____

_____

_____

4. According to Paul, what happens to those who only desire to be rich? What does he state is the "root" or source of all this evil (see verses 9–10)?

_____

_____

_____

_____

_____

_____

_____

The Good Confession (1 Timothy 6:11–16)

¹¹ But you, O man of God, flee these things and pursue righteousness, godliness, faith, love, patience, gentleness. ¹² Fight the good fight of faith, lay hold on eternal life, to which you were also called and have confessed the good confession in the presence of many witnesses. ¹³ I urge you in the sight of God who gives life to all things, and before Christ Jesus who witnessed the good confession before Pontius Pilate, ¹⁴ that you keep this commandment without spot, blameless until our Lord Jesus Christ's appearing, ¹⁵ which He will manifest in His own time, He who is the blessed and only Potentate, the King of kings and Lord of lords, ¹⁶ who alone has immortality, dwelling in unapproachable light, whom no man has seen or can see, to whom be honor and everlasting power. Amen.

5. Paul exhorts Timothy to not only reject the false teachings in the church but also to flee from the false belief that wealth brings contentment. What qualities does he state that Timothy should instead pursue? What should he seek to possess (see verses 11–12)?

6. The titles Paul bestows on God affirm God's sovereignty. What characteristics of God does Paul emphasize in this passage (see verses 15–16)?

_____

_____

_____

_____

_____

_____

_____

_____

_____

_____

_____

Instructions to the Rich (1 Timothy 6:17–21)

17 Command those who are rich in this present age not to be haughty, nor to trust in uncertain riches but in the living God, who gives us richly all things to enjoy. 18 Let them do good, that they be rich in good works, ready to give, willing to share, 19 storing up for themselves a good foundation for the time to come, that they may lay hold on eternal life.

20 O Timothy! Guard what was committed to your trust, avoiding the profane and idle babblings and contradictions of what is falsely called knowledge—21 by professing it some have strayed concerning the faith.

Grace be with you. Amen.

7. There is evidence the Ephesian church included a sizable contingent of well-to-do believers (see 2:9; 5:13). There were also slaves (see 6:1–2), widows in need (see 5:3–16), and people from all socioeconomic levels.

What is Paul's concern with this well-to-do contingent? What advice does Paul offer Timothy for discipling them (see verses 17–19)?

_____

_____

_____

_____

_____

_____

_____

8. Paul concludes with a warning against those who claimed special "knowledge" about spiritual things. What was the danger of entertaining this knowledge (see verses 20–21)?

_____

_____

_____

_____

_____

_____

_____

Reviewing the Story

Paul concludes his first letter to Timothy with a reminder that Christian bondservants can honor Christ by honoring their masters. He then reminds Timothy that false teachers are more interested in debates and arguments than in practical application. He urges Timothy to avoid their company—and also the company of those who are driven by lust and greed. Paul encourages Timothy to "fight the good fight" and to stay true to the doctrine he has received. He ends with a few instructions for the rich and a final plea for Timothy to guard the faith.

9. What does Paul say Timothy should do about the false teachers in Ephesus (see 1 Timothy 6:5)?

10. What does the love of money cause some people to do (see 1 Timothy 6:10)?

11. What phrases does Paul use to remind Timothy of whom he serves (see 1 Timothy 6:15)?

12. What is more important than building financial security
(see 1 Timothy 6:19)?

APPLYING THE MESSAGE

13. How can you pursue true contentment through righteousness,
godliness, faith, love, patience, and gentleness in your daily life?

14. What adjustments can you make in your attitude toward
material possessions?

REFLECTING ON THE MEANING

The question that should reverberate in the heart of every believer is this: "How can I become a man or woman of God?" Timothy prioritized the things of the Lord, made a difference in the lives of others, and furthered the kingdom of Christ. He earned the respect not only of the people he served but also of the people with whom he served. If we are going to do likewise, there are four things we need to keep in mind.

First, *we must be known by what we refuse to pursue.* True men and women of God are unwilling to be conformed to the "success game." The culture around us exerts a subtle yet pervasive temptation to sacrifice the truly important things—the *eternal* things—for things that do not matter in the long run. Like Timothy, we must recognize that everything we have been given represents a sacred stewardship from the almighty God.

Second, *we must be known by what we choose to pursue.* As Paul instructs Timothy, "Pursue righteousness, godliness, faith, love, patience, and gentleness" (1 Timothy 6:11). We don't wait for these qualities to suddenly show up one day. Rather, we pursue them and find ways to build them into our lives. If that means getting up a little earlier to spend time with God, or prioritizing other activities in our day to do so, then so be it.

Third, *we are known by what we choose to fight for.* We are soldiers in a spiritual war. Every day, we fight for righteousness and godliness. We put on the whole armor of God so we can stand against the evil one (see Ephesians 6:10–20). As believers, if we don't have some tension in our lives, it means something is wrong. Struggle is a good thing, because it reminds us we are spiritually alive.

Fourth, *we are known by what we are faithful to.* A man or woman of God is faithful to the Word of God. We understand that it is "profitable for doctrine, for reproof, for correction, for instruction in righteousness, that the man [and woman] of God may be complete, thoroughly equipped for every good work" (2 Timothy 3:16–17). We allow the Word of God to guide and speak into our lives, and we do not accept compromises when it comes to our faith.

JOURNALING YOUR RESPONSE

What steps will you take to grow in true contentment and godliness?

REKINDLE YOUR FAITH

2 Timothy 1:1–18

GETTING STARTED

What are some practices that you have developed to keep your faith alive and active?

_____

_____

_____

_____

_____

_____

_____

_____

_____

_____

_____

_____

_____

_____

SETTING THE STAGE

In order to fully appreciate the letter of 2 Timothy, we have to understand what happened in the two or three years since Paul sent his first letter to

Timothy. Timothy was still pastoring the church at Ephesus, but Paul was now imprisoned in a Roman dungeon, suffering "even to the point of chains" (2 Timothy 2:9). Many of Paul's friends and fellow workers had been killed in the persecution enacted by the emperor Nero. The outlook for Christians seemed dire. Paul himself would be executed shortly after sending this final letter.

Surprisingly, the emotion that comes through in the letter is not fear or regret but loneliness. Just look at some of Paul's opening words: "This you know, that all those in Asia have turned away from me, among whom are Phygellus and Hermogenes" (1:15). Later, he adds, "Demas has forsaken me, having loved this present world, and has departed for Thessalonica—Crescens for Galatia, Titus for Dalmatia" (4:10). Twice within the space of a few verses he asks Timothy to visit him (see 4:9, 21). It's a time of grim reality for the apostle. He sees the things to which he has committed his life teetering on the edge of extinction.

As for Timothy, this young man continued to be responsible for the church at Ephesus and all its sprawling daughter ministries. He was stationed in a city renowned for its wickedness and idolatry. To our knowledge, the church had little structure or organization, and the believers knew nothing about worship. It was filled with people who were older than him, many of whom likely doubted his ability to lead, based on his age.

It would not have been surprising if the circumstances Timothy faced, including the imminent execution of his spiritual father, brought about doubt and struggle in his life. So Paul is careful to offer words that will keep Timothy's faith burning.

Exploring the Text

Thanksgiving for Timothy (2 Timothy 1:1–5)

> [1] Paul, an apostle of Jesus Christ by the will of God, according to the promise of life which is in Christ Jesus,
>
> [2] To Timothy, a beloved son:

Grace, mercy, and peace from God the Father and Christ Jesus our Lord.

³ I thank God, whom I serve with a pure conscience, as my forefathers did, as without ceasing I remember you in my prayers night and day, ⁴ greatly desiring to see you, being mindful of your tears, that I may be filled with joy, ⁵ when I call to remembrance the genuine faith that is in you, which dwelt first in your grandmother Lois and your mother Eunice, and I am persuaded is in you also.

---

1. Paul was in prison, facing execution, but he still found reason to be thankful to God. What are some of the practices that Paul has maintained even in chains (see verses 3–4)?

_____

_____

_____

_____

_____

_____

_____

2. The word *genuine* that Paul uses in this passage can be also be translated *unhypocritical*. Paul recognizes that external faith can be a mask for internal bankruptcy. What are some reasons that he provides for Timothy's remarkably genuine faith (see verse 5)?

_____

_____

_____

_____

_____

Timothy's Faith and Heritage (2 Timothy 1:6–11)

⁶ Therefore I remind you to stir up the gift of God which is in you through the laying on of my hands. ⁷ For God has not given us a spirit of fear, but of power and of love and of a sound mind.

⁸ Therefore do not be ashamed of the testimony of our Lord, nor of me His prisoner, but share with me in the sufferings for the gospel according to the power of God, ⁹ who has saved us and called us with a holy calling, not according to our works, but according to His own purpose and grace which was given to us in Christ Jesus before time began, ¹⁰ but has now been revealed by the appearing of our Savior Jesus Christ, who has abolished death and brought life and immortality to light through the gospel, ¹¹ to which I was appointed a preacher, an apostle, and a teacher of the Gentiles.

3. It is likely that Timothy did not have a strong father figure in his family. As a result, he may not have been as comfortable with confrontation or dealing with opposition. What did Paul, his "spiritual father," want him to remember about his calling (see verses 6–7)?

4. Just as Jesus was deserted by His disciples before the crucifixion, so has Paul been deserted by many of his friends and fellow workers. Paul thus calls on Timothy to "share with [him] in the sufferings for the gospel" (verse 8). Why would Timothy, or anyone, want to share with Paul in the sufferings of the gospel? What was Paul's greater focus (see verses 9–10)?

_____

_____

_____

_____

_____

_____

_____

_____

_____

_____

_____

_____

Not Ashamed of the Gospel (2 Timothy 1:12–14)

12 For this reason I also suffer these things; nevertheless I am not ashamed, for I know whom I have believed and am persuaded that He is able to keep what I have committed to Him until that Day.

13 Hold fast the pattern of sound words which you have heard from me, in faith and love which are in Christ Jesus. 14 That good thing which was committed to you, keep by the Holy Spirit who dwells in us.

5. God's power overrides any earthly power. Paul knew that if Timothy understood this truth, he would align his ways of thinking with that reality rather than trust in any earthly powers. How did this mindset enable Paul to not experience any shame, even though he was imprisoned by Rome, the greatest earthly power of his day (see verse 12)?

_____

_____

_____

_____

_____

_____

_____

6. God gives a particular calling to believers, including a set of responsibilities and ultimately new life through the Holy Spirit. What is the responsibility of believers (see verses 13–14)?

_____

_____

_____

_____

_____

_____

_____

Be Loyal to the Faith (2 Timothy 1:15–18)

¹⁵ This you know, that all those in Asia have turned away from me, among whom are Phygellus and Hermogenes. ¹⁶ The Lord grant mercy to the household of Onesiphorus, for he often refreshed me, and was not ashamed of my chain; ¹⁷ but when he arrived in Rome, he sought me out very zealously and found me. ¹⁸ The Lord grant to him that he may find mercy from the Lord in that Day—and you know very well how many ways he ministered to me at Ephesus.

7. Paul's statement that many of his friends have "turned away" from him does not necessarily mean they abandoned the faith. However, it certainly means they abandoned *Paul* during his time of greatest need. How do the actions of those in the household of Onesiphorus contrast with the actions of those who deserted Paul (see verses 15–16)?

_____

_____

_____

_____

_____

_____

_____

8. When Paul wrote this letter, it is possible Onesiphorus's family was in Ephesus, while Onesiphorus himself was with Paul. What does Paul say Onesiphorus did when he arrived in Rome? What prayer does Paul have for him and his household (see verses 16–18)?

_____

_____

_____

_____

_____

_____

REVIEWING THE STORY

Paul reminds Timothy of the solid grounding he received from his mother and grandmother. He urges him to cling to that training and remember his ordination, when he was commissioned to be a pastor "through the laying on of hands" (verse 6), whenever he is feeling fearful about his ministry or the future. Paul encourages Timothy not to be ashamed of the gospel, or of him, but to join with him in embracing suffering for the sake of Christ. Paul shares his feelings of loneliness, having been abandoned by most of his companions, and expresses his gratefulness for those who are still with him. He remains resolute in his faithfulness to his Lord and Savior.

9. In what ways was Timothy equipped by God to be a disciple of Jesus (see 2 Timothy 1:1–7)?

_____

_____

_____

_____

_____

_____

10. How does Paul describe the calling that he and Timothy received (see 2 Timothy 1:9–11)?

_____

_____

_____

_____

_____

11. What help did Timothy have in keeping the sound teachings that had been entrusted to him (see 2 Timothy 1:14)?

_____

_____

_____

_____

_____

12. How did Onesiphorus serve as a role model for Timothy through his generous treatment of Paul in prison (see 2 Timothy 1:16)?

APPLYING THE MESSAGE

13. How has God equipped you to serve Him and His people?

14. How are you consistent in your faithfulness and responsibilities before God?

REFLECTING ON THE MEANING

Paul opens his second letter to Timothy by suggesting that fear is one of the biggest obstacles to revitalizing our faith. He also reminds us that fear is an unnatural reaction for believers. As he writes, "God has not given us a spirit of fear, but of power and of love and of a sound mind" (verse 7). God equips us with everything we need to serve Him. This includes *courage*—or "power," as Paul refers to it—because it takes courage to be a Christian.

Not only does Paul expect us to have courage, but he also expects us to have *compassion*. This is why God has given us a spirit of love. After all, "perfect love casts out fear" (1 John 4:18). If we start to speak to someone about our Savior and fear begins to fill our heart, we can let the love of God, which passes human understanding, fill it instead. When this happens, we become so overwhelmed with love for the person that we cannot help but speak, even if it is with stammering lips. Compassion causes us to see the other person not as a threat but as someone who needs Christ. Perfect love pushes fear right out!

Paul also encourages us to be in *control*—to have a sound mind and wise restraint. If we have the right amount of control in difficult situations, we will not bend in times of stress. We will conquer the cowardly influences that are present in ourselves. This kind of control Paul is talking about allows us to keep a constant rein on our passions and desires. It holds us in place so that our courage and compassion have a chance to do their work.

By God's design, these three traits—courage, compassion, and control—work together to create something whole within us. If we have courage without love, we could become austere. If we have courage without control, we could become extravagant in the use of our courage. If we have compassion without courage, we could sink into soft timidity. If we have compassion without control, we could become pliable and gullible. We need the presence of all three traits . . . and we need to allow God to use them in our lives.

JOURNALING YOUR RESPONSE

How do you see these three traits—courage, compassion, and control—at work in your life?

LESSON *eight*

SOLDIERS FOR CHRIST

2 Timothy 2:1–26

GETTING STARTED

How do you typically respond when you have to do something you dread?

SETTING THE STAGE

Paul opens this next section of his letter with instructions for Timothy to "endure hardship as a good soldier of Jesus Christ" (2:3). Paul approached his ministry in the same way a soldier approaches a battlefield. He knew that effective tactics, hard work, and endurance in the midst of struggles were necessary to secure the victory. Spiritually speaking, there were no gains without pains . . . no crowns without crosses. Persevering through trials leads to success.

Paul wants Timothy to thus embrace this truth and not avoid the challenges that are in his particular "battlefield." As one of Jesus' loyal soldiers, Timothy had to understand what he was facing and look to Christ for his strength. Much as in Paul's previous letter, he draws on imagery from the oppressive Roman Empire to make his point. Roman soldiers would threaten to punish any citizen who did not follow the emperor's decrees. Those in the first-century world well understood they were under Rome's authority.

However, as Paul notes, soldiers of Christ are different. They are also under the authority of a ruler, and they must be ready at all times to obey the orders of their king, but they have been given a different mission and follow different orders. Most apparent among the differences is that while the Roman soldiers would regularly *inflict* suffering on others, soldiers of Jesus will regularly *receive* and *bear* suffering from others because of their loyalty to Jesus.

This idea of enduring hardship as a good soldier of Christ is a hard reality for many of us to grasp. Religion is often considered a private matter that should not impinge on civil affairs. Yet for Paul and Timothy, serving Jesus was the focus of their lives, and it took all the strength and grace that God could provide to achieve that mission. It involved standing up for the gospel, even when that meant going against prevailing assumptions and practices of the world. The same is required of each of us today . . . and the sooner we grasp that fact, the sooner we will find ourselves able to persevere for Christ no matter what circumstances we face.

EXPLORING THE TEXT

Be Strong in Grace (2 Timothy 2:1–7)

¹ You therefore, my son, be strong in the grace that is in Christ Jesus. ² And the things that you have heard from me among many witnesses, commit these to faithful men who will be able to teach others also. ³ You therefore must endure hardship as a good soldier of Jesus Christ. ⁴ No one engaged in warfare entangles himself with the affairs of this life, that he may please him who enlisted him as a soldier. ⁵ And also if anyone competes in athletics, he is not crowned unless he competes according to the rules. ⁶ The hardworking farmer must be first to partake of the crops. ⁷ Consider what I say, and may the Lord give you understanding in all things.

1. Paul has just commented on the "sufferings for the gospel" that he has personally faced (see 1:8). He now continues this train of thought by helping Timothy understand that he will likewise face suffering in his ministry of Christ. What three instructions does Paul give to Timothy that will help him go through such trying times (see verses 1–3)?

2. Paul instructed Timothy in his first letter to "fight the good fight of faith" (1 Timothy 6:12). What three examples does Paul give to Timothy to help him understand the importance of engaging in spiritual warfare and remaining focused on Christ (see verses 4–6)?

_____

_____

_____

_____

_____

_____

_____

God's Word Is Not Chained (2 Timothy 2:8–13)

8 Remember that Jesus Christ, of the seed of David, was raised from the dead according to my gospel, 9 for which I suffer trouble as an evildoer, even to the point of chains; but the word of God is not chained. 10 Therefore I endure all things for the sake of the elect, that they also may obtain the salvation which is in Christ Jesus with eternal glory. 11 This is a faithful saying:

> For if we died with Him,
> We shall also live with Him.
> 12 If we endure,
> We shall also reign with Him.
> If we deny Him,
> He also will deny us.
> 13 If we are faithless,
> He remains faithful;
> He cannot deny Himself.

3. Paul was a Roman citizen and was innocent of the charges brought up against him of being an "evildoer." In lieu of these facts, the treatment he had received would have been recognized as an extreme indignity by all. Yet his faith did not waver. Where did Paul find the strength to persevere in the midst of his suffering (see verses 8–10)?

_____

_____

_____

_____

_____

_____

_____

4. Paul quotes yet another "faithful saying" in his letters to Timothy (see 1 Timothy 1:15; 3:1; 4:9). This particular saying continues Paul's point that serving Christ involves suffering. What incredible promise does he provide in this passage (see 2 Timothy 2:11–13)?

_____

_____

_____

_____

_____

_____

_____

Approved and Disapproved Workers (2 Timothy 2:14–19)

14 Remind them of these things, charging them before the Lord not to strive about words to no profit, to the ruin of the hearers. 15 Be diligent to present yourself approved to God, a worker who does not need to be ashamed, rightly dividing the word of truth. 16 But shun profane and idle babblings, for they will increase to more ungodliness. 17 And their message will spread like cancer. Hymenaeus and Philetus are

of this sort, [18] who have strayed concerning the truth, saying that the resurrection is already past; and they overthrow the faith of some. [19] Nevertheless the solid foundation of God stands, having this seal: "The Lord knows those who are His," and, "Let everyone who names the name of Christ depart from iniquity."

---

5. Paul instructs Timothy to remind his congregation of these truths and be like diligent workers for Christ. His reference to a workman in this instance suggests someone who is skilled and properly trained. How can someone who knows how to rightly divide "the word of truth" make an impact on other people's lives (see verses 14–16)?

_____

_____

_____

_____

_____

6. Paul previously noted that Hymenaeus was a dangerous false teacher in the church whom he had "handed over to Satan to be taught not to blaspheme" (1 Timothy 1:20). Philetus is not mentioned elsewhere, but it is clear that both men were engaging in heresy. What was their particular heresy? What effect was it having on the church (see 2 Timothy 2:17–18)?

_____

_____

_____

_____

_____

Vessels for God's Use (2 Timothy 2:20–26)

20 But in a great house there are not only vessels of gold and silver, but also of wood and clay, some for honor and some for dishonor. 21 Therefore if anyone cleanses himself from the latter, he will be a vessel for honor, sanctified and useful for the Master, prepared for every good work. 22 Flee also youthful lusts; but pursue righteousness, faith, love, peace with those who call on the Lord out of a pure heart. 23 But avoid foolish and ignorant disputes, knowing that they generate strife. 24 And a servant of the Lord must not quarrel but be gentle to all, able to teach, patient, 25 in humility correcting those who are in opposition, if God perhaps will grant them repentance, so that they may know the truth, 26 and that they may come to their senses and escape the snare of the devil, having been taken captive by him to do his will.

7. Vessels of gold and silver and vessels of wood and clay all have their purposes in the home. However, as Paul notes here, some purposes are more noble than others. Why is it important for believers to be cleansed from dishonorable purposes (see verses 20–21)?

8. One of the best ways to make ourselves useful to God is to recognize the things that have lasting value in our lives and choose to pursue those things. What does Paul say that we are to flee? What does Paul say we should pursue instead (see verses 22–26)?

_____

_____

_____

_____

_____

_____

REVIEWING THE STORY

Paul urges Timothy to embrace his place in the line of gospel teachers by taking what he had learned from Paul—and what Paul had learned from Christ's example—and passing it on to those who would pass it on to others. Paul uses the examples of a soldier, an athlete, and a farmer to help Timothy understand his mission and what hardships he can expect to face along the way. Paul emphasizes that though he is in chains, bound in a Roman prison, the gospel message that he is proclaiming cannot be bound. He implores Timothy to become an expert in God's Word and to tirelessly pursue the example of Jesus Christ.

9. What did Paul pray that God would give to Timothy (see 2 Timothy 2:7)?

_____

_____

_____

_____

_____

10. What promises does Paul encourage Timothy to cling to during times of trial for strength and encouragement (see 2 Timothy 2:11–13)?

11. Why did Paul use Hymenaeus and Philetus as examples of the path Timothy needed to avoid (see 2 Timothy 2:17–18)?

12. Why is it important for a servant of God to possess a gentle spirit, an ability to teach, patience, humility, and a willingness to correct false doctrine (see 2 Timothy 2:23–26)?

APPLYING THE MESSAGE

13. In what ways can you put Paul's instructions in this passage into practice right now?

_____

_____

_____

_____

_____

_____

_____

_____

_____

_____

14. How would you like to grow as a servant of Jesus Christ?

_____

_____

_____

_____

_____

_____

_____

_____

_____

_____

_____

REFLECTING ON THE MEANING

In this section of Paul's letter, he is clear in telling Timothy the life of a Christian minister is not for the faint of heart. He goes on to stress exactly what will be required of those who "enlist" in God's army and choose this path. Paul supports these requirements with four illustrations that apply to all of us who seek to fulfill God's calling and be His servants.

First, *we are to be teachers who communicate the truth* (see verse 2). Paul saw Timothy as a link in the chain of the continuation of the gospel message. He said to him, in effect, "Just as I received my message from Christ, and as you have received that message from me, you are to take it to faithful people who, in turn, will teach it to others."

Second, *we are to be soldiers who fight spiritual battles* (see verse 3). Paul wants the discipline of the military to find its way into Timothy's life. He wants Timothy to be able to endure difficulty and to have the intensity and diligence to pursue the goals of his Commander . . . even when it involves hardships.

Third, *we are to be athletes who train for the prize* (see verse 5). When a Greek runner finished first in the Olympiad, the judges would determine whether he had run that race according to the rules. If he had, they would then award the prize. Paul is telling Timothy, in effect, "Keep the rules of discipline—the rules that apply to everyone who serves Christ."

Fourth, *we are to be farmers who sow the seeds of the gospel* (see verse 6). Farmers do not just go out, throw the seed randomly on the ground, and then come back a few months later and hope to see a crop. Rather, they invest themselves in realizing a good harvest. Farmers are willing to do this even when no one is watching, for they know that one day the fruit of their labors will be known to all when the crop is harvested.

Servants of Jesus are to visibly communicate their loyalty to their King and to God's kingdom. At the same time, some of the most important tasks in God's kingdom are those that nobody sees. This is the real test of a true servant of Jesus. Do we shine just as brightly for Him when nobody else is watching?

JOURNALING YOUR RESPONSE

Which of Paul's four illustrations hits closest to home for you? Explain.

A LIFE WORTHY OF IMITATION

2 Timothy 3:1–17

GETTING STARTED

Who has set the best example of godliness for you? How did that person set an example?

_____

_____

_____

_____

_____

_____

_____

_____

_____

_____

_____

_____

SETTING THE STAGE

The apostle Paul has called on believers to be a "vessel for honor" for Christ, pursuing "righteousness, faith, love, [and] peace" (2:22). He will now describe the situation that occurs when people *do not* seek to be such vessels for honor. In particular, he will speak about the evil that will fill the world during the end times, when people are boastful and malignant, corrupting everything they encounter. Paul states that an attitude will arise in which people view themselves as having a form of godliness . . . but they will have no power from God.

Paul calls for Timothy to be different. He is to stand apart from the world and stand up for what he believes. Just as the false teachers that Paul identifies were to be recognized and understood by the way they lived, so true believers in Christ are to be recognized and understood by the way they live. Doctrine should translate into everyday conduct.

It has been said that in Christian ministry, if you communicate from your head, you might change someone's mind. If you communicate from your heart, you might change someone's attitude. But if you communicate from your *life*, you might change someone's life. This is Paul's message to Timothy . . . and to us. He reveals what happens when we communicate to others based on the way we live our lives.

It is interesting that Paul says to Timothy, "You have carefully followed my doctrine" (3:10). In this context, *followed* can refer to walking alongside someone or following in someone's footsteps, but it can also refer to imitating the spiritual example of someone. Paul is saying to Timothy, "You watched me and saw how I lived. You know who I am because I've been vulnerable with you. Now follow my example . . . and *be* an example to someone else."

EXPLORING THE TEXT

Perilous Times and Perilous Men (2 Timothy 3:1–5)

¹ But know this, that in the last days perilous times will come: ² For men will be lovers of themselves, lovers of money, boasters, proud, blasphemers, disobedient to parents, unthankful, unholy, ³ unloving, unforgiving, slanderers, without self-control, brutal, despisers of

good, ⁴ traitors, headstrong, haughty, lovers of pleasure rather than lovers of God, ⁵ having a form of godliness but denying its power. And from such people turn away!

1. Paul opens by putting the moral decay that is presently at work in the world into perspective. What does Paul say that people will be like in the last days (see verses 1–5)? Why might this actually give Timothy *hope* when he encounters people who do evil?

_____

_____

_____

_____

_____

2. The types of people Paul includes have one thing in common— *godless self-centeredness*. What was Paul's advice to Timothy concerning these dangerous people (see verse 5)?

_____

_____

_____

_____

_____

_____

_____

Opponents of the Truth (2 Timothy 3:6–9)

⁶ For of this sort are those who creep into households and make captives of gullible women loaded down with sins, led away by various lusts, ⁷ always learning and never able to come to the knowledge of

the truth. ⁸ Now as Jannes and Jambres resisted Moses, so do these also resist the truth: men of corrupt minds, disapproved concerning the faith; ⁹ but they will progress no further, for their folly will be manifest to all, as theirs also was.

3. In a Greek home, it was possible for a man to join the household by getting approval from the mistress of the house to serve as a teacher for the children. Perhaps this was how the men to whom Paul is referring were able to "creep into households." Who were the targets of these deceitful false teachers? How does Paul describe them (see verses 6–7)?

_____

_____

_____

_____

_____

4. According to Jewish tradition, Jannes and Jambres were the two Egyptian magicians in Exodus 7 who threw down their staves and transformed them into snakes. What are the similarities between these men and those with whom Timothy is dealing (see verses 8–9)?

_____

_____

_____

_____

_____

The Man of God and the Word of God (2 Timothy 3:10–13)

¹⁰ But you have carefully followed my doctrine, manner of life, purpose, faith, longsuffering, love, perseverance, ¹¹ persecutions,

afflictions, which happened to me at Antioch, at Iconium, at Lystra—
what persecutions I endured. And out of them all the Lord delivered
me. ¹²Yes, and all who desire to live godly in Christ Jesus will suffer
persecution. ¹³But evil men and impostors will grow worse and
worse, deceiving and being deceived.

---

5. Paul had suffered much persecution in his work of spreading
the gospel, yet the Lord never abandoned him. What was the most
important thing the apostle wanted Timothy to take away from the
many persecutions that Paul had endured (see verses 10–11)?

_____

_____

_____

_____

_____

6. Paul's words in this passage echo those of Jesus to His own followers:
"If they persecuted Me, they will also persecute you" (John 15:20). If we
follow Paul's example and work to live a godly life in Christ Jesus, what
can we also expect (see verses 12–13)?

_____

_____

_____

_____

_____

All Scripture Is Profitable (2 Timothy 3:14–17)

---

¹⁴But you must continue in the things which you have learned and
been assured of, knowing from whom you have learned them,

¹⁵ and that from childhood you have known the Holy Scriptures, which are able to make you wise for salvation through faith which is in Christ Jesus.

¹⁶ All Scripture is given by inspiration of God, and is profitable for doctrine, for reproof, for correction, for instruction in righteousness, ¹⁷ that the man of God may be complete, thoroughly equipped for every good work.

---

7. Paul stresses that as the false teachers continue in their downward trajectory, so Timothy must continue to grow upward in his faith. Why does Paul say Timothy is able to remain confident in the things he has "learned and been assured of" (see verses 14–15)?

_____

_____

_____

_____

_____

8. Paul states Scripture is profitable for doctrine, reproof, correction, and instruction. *Doctrine* is teaching, *reproof* is conviction, *correction* is setting someone straight, and *instruction* (as Paul uses the term here) refers to training in spiritual matters. If believers embrace all four aspects of Scripture, what will be the result (see verses 16–17)?

_____

_____

_____

_____

_____

REVIEWING THE STORY

Paul offers Timothy a snapshot of the kinds of people there will be in the end times. He urges Timothy to consider the way people live and avoid those whose lives aren't worthy of imitation. In contrast, Paul offers his own life as a model Timothy should follow, because he worked hard to provide people with a living example of what it meant to follow Christ. Paul urges Timothy to hold fast to everything he has been taught and shown—especially the Word of God.

9. What specific types of people does Paul warn Timothy to avoid (see 2 Timothy 3:2–5)?

_____

_____

_____

_____

_____

_____

_____

10. What does Paul say will prevent the false teachers in Ephesus from progressing any further in their damaging ministry (see 2 Timothy 3:9)?

_____

_____

_____

_____

_____

_____

11. What did Paul want Timothy to remember when it came to persecutions and afflictions (see 2 Timothy 3:10–11)?

_____

_____

_____

_____

12. What did Paul say that Scripture (the Word of God) could do for Timothy and for anyone else who aspires to be a man or woman of God (see 2 Timothy 3:17)?

_____

_____

_____

_____

Applying the Message

13. What would happen if a young Christian followed the example you have set in your life?

_____

_____

_____

_____

_____

14. What changes need to be made in your life in order to be able to say with confidence, as Paul did, "Follow my example"?

_____

_____

_____

_____

_____

REFLECTING ON THE MEANING

Timothy, like an apprentice, had been given the opportunity to watch Paul up close. He had observed what Paul endured and how the apostle remained faithful in every situation. In this section, Paul lists several ways that he had communicated his faith and his character to Timothy.

First, *he communicated truth through practice and purpose* (see verse 10). When Paul first visited Lystra, where Timothy lived, he angered certain people. They threw stones at Paul and dragged him outside the city. Before long, however, Paul came back and preached the same gospel that had gotten him into trouble. Timothy observed that Paul was committed to a *purpose* that was greater than his own life. And as he continued to watch, he saw that Paul was committed to practicing what he preached. We must likewise be a godly example to others.

Second, *the apostle Paul communicated truth through perseverance and longsuffering* (see verse 10). Paul didn't move away from the doctrine he believed when it was tested. He didn't water it down to make it less offensive to people who objected to it. Instead, he patiently persevered through every circumstance and held up the Word of God as absolute truth. Paul's own patience is the reason he could instruct Timothy to "be gentle to all, able to teach, patient, in humility correcting those who are in opposition, if God perhaps will grant them repentance, so that they may know the truth" (2:24–25).

Finally, *Paul communicated truth through persecutions and afflictions* (3:11). Paul had been driven out of Pisidian Antioch (see Acts 13:50). He had to flee from Iconium to avoid a plot there against his life (see 14:5). Timothy knew about each of these experiences. He had learned from Paul's example that crisis builds character and reveals the kind of people we are in Christ.

Paul knew the time had come for Timothy to stand firm in the truth that he had learned. Life would not be easy for him, but with the Word of God in his heart and mind, he would be able to grow in faith and train others in faith as well. The same is true for us.

JOURNALING YOUR RESPONSE

Why is it essential as a believer in Christ to practice what you preach?

AWAITING THE CROWN

2 Timothy 4:1–22

GETTING STARTED

What are some goals that you are looking forward to realizing in your life?

_____

_____

_____

_____

_____

_____

_____

_____

_____

_____

_____

_____

_____

_____

_____

_____

_____

_____

_____

_____

SETTING THE STAGE

In this final section of Paul's letter, we find his last words to his beloved son in the faith, Timothy, and to the church. As he completes the letter, Paul knows his execution is only days or weeks away. For thirty years, he has labored as an apostle, a preacher, and an evangelist. He summarizes his mission by stating he has fought the good fight, finished the course laid out before him, and kept the faith. He is now looking forward to the reward that awaits him.

However, Paul has a few final instructions to offer before he takes that journey. We can sense the increasing urgency in his words—a staccato-like set of imperatives to *preach, convince, rebuke, exhort, teach, watch,* and *endure* (see verses 2, 5). Paul wants Timothy to know *exactly* what he must do if he is to be a faithful minister of the gospel.

Paul had previously emphasized to Timothy the importance of preserving the doctrine he had received. Now Paul says, in effect, "It's not enough to just *hold* the truth. You must *herald* the truth as well." In other words, it's not enough for us to just believe what we believe. We must also be willing to declare what we believe.

Paul's words remind us that we never know how close we are to our last day on earth. So, we must live each day being ready to give an account of our lives. If we have received a calling, we need to get on with it. It may be difficult and painful at times, but we can know that it will all be worth it when we see Jesus and receive our "crown of righteousness" (verse 8).

EXPLORING THE TEXT

Preach the Word (2 Timothy 4:1–5)

> [1] I charge you therefore before God and the Lord Jesus Christ, who will judge the living and the dead at His appearing and His kingdom: [2] Preach the word! Be ready in season and out of season. Convince, rebuke, exhort, with all longsuffering and teaching. [3] For

the time will come when they will not endure sound doctrine, but according to their own desires, because they have itching ears, they will heap up for themselves teachers; [4] and they will turn their ears away from the truth, and be turned aside to fables. [5] But you be watchful in all things, endure afflictions, do the work of an evangelist, fulfill your ministry.

---

1. When Paul told Timothy to "preach the word" (verse 2), the New Testament had not yet been completely written or assembled into the canon of Scripture that we recognize today. So what might he be referring to in his instruction to preach "the word" (see verses 1–2)?

_____

_____

_____

_____

_____

_____

_____

2. What does Paul say people will do when they don't want to hear the truth of the gospel? In contrast, how should Timothy—and all believers—respond to the gospel (see verses 3–5)?

_____

_____

_____

_____

_____

_____

Paul's Valedictory (2 Timothy 4:6–8)

> ⁶ For I am already being poured out as a drink offering, and the time of my departure is at hand. ⁷ I have fought the good fight, I have finished the race, I have kept the faith. ⁸ Finally, there is laid up for me the crown of righteousness, which the Lord, the righteous Judge, will give to me on that Day, and not to me only but also to all who have loved His appearing.

3. Paul's statement that he is "being poured out as a drink offering" is a reference to his impending death. What knowledge comforted him as he faced this fact (see verses 6–7)?

_____

_____

_____

_____

_____

_____

_____

4. Paul describes himself as a runner at the end of a race. It is all but over, and what remains is the rewarding of the prize. What did he see at the finish line (see verses 7–8)?

_____

_____

_____

_____

_____

_____

The Abandoned Apostle (2 Timothy 4:9–16)

⁹ Be diligent to come to me quickly; ¹⁰ for Demas has forsaken me, having loved this present world, and has departed for Thessalonica—Crescens for Galatia, Titus for Dalmatia. ¹¹ Only Luke is with me. Get Mark and bring him with you, for he is useful to me for ministry. ¹² And Tychicus I have sent to Ephesus. ¹³ Bring the cloak that I left with Carpus at Troas when you come—and the books, especially the parchments.

¹⁴ Alexander the coppersmith did me much harm. May the Lord repay him according to his works. ¹⁵ You also must beware of him, for he has greatly resisted our words.

¹⁶ At my first defense no one stood with me, but all forsook me. May it not be charged against them.

5. In the Gospels, we read that all of Jesus' disciples "forsook Him and fled" when He was arrested by the Roman authorities (Mark 14:50). Shortly after, Jesus exclaimed from the cross, "My God, My God, why have You forsaken Me?" (15:34). What parallels do you see between Jesus' experience and Paul's experience (see 2 Timothy 4:9–13)?

6. As Jesus was hanging on the cross, He prayed for those who crucified Him, "Father, forgive them, for they do not know what they do" (Luke 23:34). What parallels do you see between Jesus' response and Paul's response to those who abandoned them (see 2 Timothy 4:16)?

_____

_____

_____

_____

_____

_____

_____

_____

_____

_____

_____

The Lord Is Faithful (2 Timothy 4:17–22)

¹⁷ But the Lord stood with me and strengthened me, so that the message might be preached fully through me, and that all the Gentiles might hear. Also I was delivered out of the mouth of the lion. ¹⁸ And the Lord will deliver me from every evil work and preserve me for His heavenly kingdom. To Him be glory forever and ever. Amen!

¹⁹ Greet Prisca and Aquila, and the household of Onesiphorus. ²⁰ Erastus stayed in Corinth, but Trophimus I have left in Miletus sick.

²¹ Do your utmost to come before winter.

Eubulus greets you, as well as Pudens, Linus, Claudia, and all the brethren.

²² The Lord Jesus Christ be with your spirit. Grace be with you. Amen.

7. Paul experienced multiple occasions where the Lord spoke to him and gave him specific instructions (see, for example, Acts 22:17–21; 23:11). What blessing did Paul enjoy throughout his ministry . . . even to the very end (see 2 Timothy 4:17)?

_____

_____

_____

_____

_____

_____

_____

_____

8. Based on Paul's countless past experiences, what is he confident the Lord will do for him (see verse 18)?

_____

_____

_____

_____

_____

_____

_____

REVIEWING THE STORY

In Paul's final words to Timothy, he reminds his younger protégé of his primary responsibility: to preach the gospel of Jesus Christ. Paul warns Timothy that his message may not always be welcomed—that people won't always want to hear the truth. But he encourages Timothy not to let this stop him. Paul then reflects on his ministry with a sense of accomplishment and finality. He pleads for Timothy to visit him, for everyone has abandoned him, and concludes his letter with a heartfelt farewell to his son in the faith. Paul is beset by difficulties, yet he remains determined to bring every aspect of his life under the gospel and bring glory to Christ. He lives in Caesar's world, but he is already a joyful citizen of the world that is to come.

9. What should a believer in Christ always be ready to do (see 2 Timothy 4:2)?

_____

_____

_____

_____

_____

_____

_____

_____

10. How does Paul describe his impending death (see 2 Timothy 4:6)?

_____

_____

_____

_____

_____

_____

_____

_____

11. Paul and Barnabas had ended their partnership over a dispute about John Mark, who had left at one point in their journey (see Acts 13:13; 15:36–41). What does Paul indicate had changed about Mark? What does he request regarding him (see 2 Timothy 4:11)?

_____

_____

_____

_____

_____

_____

12. What did Paul recognize was the ultimate purpose of his life (see 2 Timothy 4:17)?

_____

_____

_____

_____

_____

_____

APPLYING THE MESSAGE

13. How do you typically respond when you feel abandoned by others?

_____

_____

_____

_____

_____

_____

14. How has God made His presence known to you during such times?

_____

_____

_____

_____

_____

REFLECTING ON THE MEANING

This final section of Paul's letter to Timothy constitutes his last recorded words in the New Testament. Paul understood he was "already being poured out as a drink offering" (4:6) and that his life on this earth would soon be coming to an end. He could now look back at the race he had run and look forward to the reward he would soon receive. But before he left, he had a final challenge for his beloved son in the faith: "Preach the word!" (verse 2).

It is little wonder this was Paul's final instruction to Timothy. After all, Jesus' final instruction was to "go into all the world and preach the gospel to every creature" (Mark 16:15). Paul had wholeheartedly accepted this challenge. His desire was now for Timothy—and for us—to continue this mission to proclaim the good news of Christ to a lost and hurting world.

Paul then states how this "preaching of the Word" should be accomplished. First, we are to "convince, rebuke, exhort" (verse 2). Sometimes, we appeal to the intellect of our hearers by convincing them. Other times, we appeal to the morality of our listeners by rebuking them. Still other times, we appeal to the emotions of our recipients by exhorting them. We do this "with all longsuffering" (verse 2), which means we are always patient. We do not simply tell people what they are doing wrong but teach them to do what is right.

Furthermore, we continue to preach the Word even when faced with people who "will not endure sound doctrine" (verse 3). The reality is that we will encounter people who do not want to hear what God says about the way they should live. These people only want to hear from teachers who appeal to their "itching ears." When that happens, Paul says to us, "Just keep doing what you're doing. Press on toward the goal. Fight the good fight. Finish the race. And one day, you will receive the crown of righteousness" (see verses 7–8).

JOURNALING YOUR RESPONSE

Now that you have finished reading 1 and 2 Timothy, how have you been challenged to live your life worthy of the gospel?

GOD'S PLAN

Titus 1:1–16

GETTING STARTED

If you were in charge of choosing a leader for a new ministry in your church, where would you start your search?

_____

_____

_____

_____

_____

_____

_____

_____

_____

_____

_____

_____

_____

SETTING THE STAGE

The Bible tells us little about Titus, aside from the fact he was a companion of the apostle Paul. In Galatians, we read that Titus accompanied Paul when he went to Jerusalem to present the gospel he was proclaiming (see 2:1–3). Although he is not mentioned in Acts, he surfaces in Paul's letters as a trusted member of his inner circle (see 2 Corinthians 2:12–13; 7:5–6; 8:6). In this respect, Titus shared something in common with Timothy.

It is no surprise, then, that in Paul's short letter to Titus, we find the same warm language and personal tone that we find in his letters to Timothy. As pastors, Titus and Timothy shared a rare bond with Paul. They were doing the essential "grunt work" of turning a group of individual believers into a cohesive whole—something infinitely greater than the sum of its parts. They were shaping the Christian church as we know it today.

Paul deeply respected Titus—whom he called "a true son in our common faith" (1:4)—and chose him to lead the church he founded on the island of Crete. Yet Paul knew he would face enormous challenges there. As with most first-century congregations, the church faced problems unique to its location. Crete was a prosperous business center, which fostered greed and consumption. It wasn't long before those vices made their way into the church. Certain people of influence were finding ways to enjoy personal gain by tweaking certain doctrines.

In Paul's opening words to Titus, he calls out these false teachers, shines a light on their motives, and exposes the damage they are causing. He then identifies the characteristics and qualities necessary for church elders and contrasts them with the characteristics and qualities of the false teachers. In doing so, Paul introduces his theme: *godliness*, the evidence of the Lord's work in a believer's life. The love of Christ within us finds its way out of us through good works. The presence of good works in our lives speaks volumes about the One we follow.

EXPLORING THE TEXT

Greeting (Titus 1:1–4)

¹ Paul, a bondservant of God and an apostle of Jesus Christ, according to the faith of God's elect and the acknowledgment of the truth

which accords with godliness, [2] in hope of eternal life which God, who cannot lie, promised before time began, [3] but has in due time manifested His word through preaching, which was committed to me according to the commandment of God our Savior;

[4] To Titus, a true son in our common faith:

Grace, mercy, and peace from God the Father and the Lord Jesus Christ our Savior.

---

1. Paul's phrase, "God's elect," links New Testament believers with God's "chosen people" of the Old Testament. In this introductory greeting, how does Paul describe the purpose of his ministry within the framework of God's overall plan (see verses 1–3)?

_____

_____

_____

_____

_____

_____

2. Paul was a Jew, while Titus was a Gentile. What bond does Paul imply was far stronger than their cultural differences (see verse 4)?

_____

_____

_____

_____

_____

_____

Qualified Elders (Titus 1:5–9)

⁵ For this reason I left you in Crete, that you should set in order the things that are lacking, and appoint elders in every city as I commanded you—⁶ if a man is blameless, the husband of one wife, having faithful children not accused of dissipation or insubordination. ⁷ For a bishop must be blameless, as a steward of God, not self-willed, not quick-tempered, not given to wine, not violent, not greedy for money, ⁸ but hospitable, a lover of what is good, sober-minded, just, holy, self-controlled, ⁹ holding fast the faithful word as he has been taught, that he may be able, by sound doctrine, both to exhort and convict those who contradict.

3. Paul had previously passed through Crete on his voyage to Rome (see Acts 27:7–13), and tradition holds that after his release, he returned there and left Titus in charge of the congregation. What were Titus's primary responsibilities in Crete (see Titus 1:5)?

4. Paul's list of qualifications for elders is nearly identical to the list of qualifications for bishops in 1 Timothy 3:1–7. In what areas of life must elders be blameless (see verses 6–9)?

_____

_____

_____

_____

_____

_____

The Problems in Crete (Titus 1:10–12)

[10] For there are many insubordinate, both idle talkers and deceivers, especially those of the circumcision, [11] whose mouths must be stopped, who subvert whole households, teaching things which they ought not, for the sake of dishonest gain. [12] One of them, a prophet of their own, said, "Cretans are always liars, evil beasts, lazy gluttons."

5. Paul's final qualification leads him to explain why "sound doctrine" is essential. What were some of the problems the members of the church in Crete faced (see verse 10)?

_____

_____

_____

_____

_____

_____

6. Paul does not advise Titus to patiently confront the "idle talkers and deceivers." Rather, he instructs that their "mouths must be stopped." What impact were these people's false teachings having on church members in Crete (see verses 11–12)?

_____

_____

_____

_____

_____

The Elders' Task (Titus 1:13–16)

¹³ This testimony is true. Therefore rebuke them sharply, that they may be sound in the faith, ¹⁴ not giving heed to Jewish fables and commandments of men who turn from the truth. ¹⁵ To the pure all things are pure, but to those who are defiled and unbelieving nothing is pure; but even their mind and conscience are defiled. ¹⁶ They profess to know God, but in works they deny Him, being abominable, disobedient, and disqualified for every good work.

7. While the exact nature of the heresy being proclaimed in Crete is not known, Paul's use of the term "Jewish fables" implies the false teachers were twisting some details of the Old Testament law to make their claims. What danger did Paul see in this teaching? What did he advise Titus to do to counter its impact in the congregation (see verses 13–14)?

_____

_____

_____

_____

8. Paul states it is the condition of our heart that matters. If we desire to do good, then good things will result. But if we desire to do evil, then evil will result. What does Paul say were the desires of people's hearts in Crete? What was the result (see verses 15–16)?

_____

_____

_____

_____

_____

_____

REVIEWING THE STORY

Paul opens his letter by reminding Titus why he was appointed to pastor in Crete: "[to] set in order the things that are lacking, and appoint elders" (Titus 1:5). Paul goes on to list the characteristics that Titus should look for in prospective elders and states that above all, such individuals should hold on to the sound doctrine of the faith they have been taught. Paul explains that the reason it is so important for Titus to choose good elders is because there are those in the church who are twisting this doctrine for their own gain, and he needs leaders who will counteract their influence. Paul closes by urging Titus to be shrewd in identifying these false teachers—"Whose mouths must be stopped" (verse 11)—and sharp in his rebuke of them.

9. What blessing does Paul ask God to give to Titus (see Titus 1:4)?

_____

_____

_____

_____

_____

10. Why was it essential for a bishop to hold fast to sound doctrine (see Titus 1:9)?

_____

_____

_____

_____

_____

_____

_____

11. What quote does Paul use to warn Titus about false teachers (see Titus 1:12)?

_____

_____

_____

_____

_____

_____

12. How does Paul say that believers recognize false teachers (see Titus 1:16)?

_____

_____

_____

_____

_____

_____

_____

APPLYING THE MESSAGE

13. What are some of the roles that you have been given in the church?

_____

_____

_____

_____

_____

_____

_____

_____

14. What does it mean for you to follow and promote "sound doctrine"?

_____

_____

_____

_____

_____

_____

_____

_____

REFLECTING ON THE MEANING

Paul begins his letter to Titus by making an interesting observation: "To the pure all things are pure, but to those who are defiled and unbelieving nothing is pure; but even their mind and conscience are defiled" (1:15). The false teachers in Crete were twisting the sound doctrine they had received and creating a new doctrine for themselves based on works. Paul wanted Titus to understand the myths they were proclaiming and rebuke them sharply.

Today, we likewise need to understand the role good works play in our lives as believers and identify three keys myths about them. First, *good works never result in salvation*. In a later section of Paul's letter, he will write, "When the kindness and the love of God our Savior toward man appeared, not by works of righteousness which we have done, but according to His mercy He saved us" (3:4–5). God sees us as righteous solely because of what Jesus did, not because of anything we have done. Salvation only comes by accepting Him as our Savior and Lord.

Second, *good works are still necessary*. Before God sent Jesus into the world, people lived under the Law of Moses. They obeyed God's commands and offered the necessary sacrifices to atone for their sins and be declared righteous. When Jesus came, He fulfilled the law in its entirety and initiated a new covenant. But this act of grace did not cancel our responsibility to live and behave in a certain way. Paul is clear about this point when he states the qualifications that those in Crete must possess if they wish to be elders (see 1:5–9).

Third, *good works won't always come naturally for us*. When we accept Jesus as our Savior, it immediately changes our standing before God. We become new people, spiritually speaking, and the Holy Spirit enters our hearts and begins to exert His influence on our lives. But this does not eliminate our sinful nature. We will still be tempted to act according to our former way of life. Godliness is something that grows within us . . . and it all begins with the attitude of our heart (see verses 15–16).

In the end, we find there is a cyclical relationship between works and godliness. Good works can never save us or impact the way God sees us. However, as we *do* good to others, it allows the Holy Spirit to work in our lives. He begins to change our attitudes, our motivations, our outlook on life, and our priorities as we put the needs of others before our own. In time, we grow in our faith and become closer to the One who created us to do good works.

Journaling Your Response

What are some of the "good works" that you like to do for others?

GOD'S AMAZING GRACE

Titus 2:1–3:15

GETTING STARTED

When have you received a gift from someone you mistreated? How did you respond?

SETTING THE STAGE

The remainder of Paul's letter to Titus focuses on *grace* . . . both receiving it from God and giving it to others. Paul begins with a discussion on how the church members in Crete should be showing love to one another and the qualities they should possess as a result. These character traits should be true of *everyone*—older men and women, younger men and women, servants and masters—and, when present, indicate the church is spiritually sound and growing.

Paul's life had forever been transformed when he experienced "the grace of God" that "has appeared to all men" (Titus 2:11). Paul understood this gift of grace from God has value for us in the *present*, for it teaches us to deny ungodliness and live righteously in this age. In fact, the Greek word he uses for *appeared* is the same from which we derive the word *epiphany*. The Greeks used it to explain what happens when the sun bursts into the darkness and brings forth the dawn. Paul always used it in his letters to describe the coming of Jesus in the world. Jesus was the living, breathing, embodiment of God's incredible grace.

Paul's message to Titus—and to us—is that because of God's grace, we can now "become heirs according to the hope of eternal life" (3:7). Thus, God's gift of grace also has value for us in the *future*. It is only because of God's grace—and "not by works of righteousness which we have done" (verse 5)—that we are able to obtain eternal life. As John Newton famously put it in his hymn *Amazing Grace*, "The earth shall soon dissolve like snow, the sun forbear to shine. But God, who called me here below, will be forever mine."

EXPLORING THE TEXT

Qualities of a Sound Church (Titus 2:1–8)

¹ But as for you, speak the things which are proper for sound doctrine:

² that the older men be sober, reverent, temperate, sound in faith, in

love, in patience; ³ the older women likewise, that they be reverent in behavior, not slanderers, not given to much wine, teachers of good things—⁴ that they admonish the young women to love their husbands, to love their children, ⁵ to be discreet, chaste, homemakers, good, obedient to their own husbands, that the word of God may not be blasphemed.

⁶ Likewise, exhort the young men to be sober-minded, ⁷ in all things showing yourself to be a pattern of good works; in doctrine showing integrity, reverence, incorruptibility, ⁸ sound speech that cannot be condemned, that one who is an opponent may be ashamed, having nothing evil to say of you.

1. Paul begins by making apparent the difference that should exist between the false teachers in Crete and Titus as a preacher of the true Word of God. As a pastor, what was Titus's responsibility in maintaining a God-honoring church (see verses 1–5)?

2. Many of the young people in the Cretan church, just as in the church today, lacked models of mature believers to teach them how to live the Christian life. What role did mentoring play in Paul's instructions to Titus regarding the young men in the church (see verses 6–8)?

_____

_____

_____

_____

_____

_____

_____

_____

_____

_____

Trained by Saving Grace (Titus 2:9–15)

⁹ Exhort bondservants to be obedient to their own masters, to be well pleasing in all things, not answering back, ¹⁰ not pilfering, but showing all good fidelity, that they may adorn the doctrine of God our Savior in all things.

¹¹ For the grace of God that brings salvation has appeared to all men, ¹² teaching us that, denying ungodliness and worldly lusts, we should live soberly, righteously, and godly in the present age, ¹³ looking for the blessed hope and glorious appearing of our great God and Savior Jesus Christ, ¹⁴ who gave Himself for us, that He might redeem us from every lawless deed and purify for Himself His own special people, zealous for good works.

¹⁵ Speak these things, exhort, and rebuke with all authority. Let no one despise you.

3. As previously noted, bondservants, or slaves, made up a large portion of the population of the ancient world—and thus of the church. What instructions does Paul give to this group on how they are to act? Why do you think Paul would advise them to do this (see verses 9–10)?

_____

_____

_____

_____

_____

_____

_____

_____

_____

_____

4. Playing on this theme of "bondservants," Paul notes that God's grace does not give us license to total freedom. How should a correct understanding of God's grace affect the way we live? What should inspire us as we work to lead godly lives (see verses 11–14)?

_____

_____

_____

_____

_____

_____

_____

_____

_____

Graces of the Heirs of Grace (Titus 3:1–8)

¹ Remind them to be subject to rulers and authorities, to obey, to be ready for every good work, ² to speak evil of no one, to be peaceable, gentle, showing all humility to all men. ³ For we ourselves were also once foolish, disobedient, deceived, serving various lusts and pleasures, living in malice and envy, hateful and hating one another. ⁴ But when the kindness and the love of God our Savior toward man appeared, ⁵ not by works of righteousness which we have done, but according to His mercy He saved us, through the washing of regeneration and renewing of the Holy Spirit, ⁶ whom He poured out on us abundantly through Jesus Christ our Savior, ⁷ that having been justified by His grace we should become heirs according to the hope of eternal life.

⁸ This is a faithful saying, and these things I want you to affirm constantly, that those who have believed in God should be careful to maintain good works. These things are good and profitable to men.

5. Paul now reveals that God's transforming grace should impact not only our interactions within the church but also our interactions with the outside world. How does Paul say we should treat those in authority? How should this extend to everyone (see verses 1–2)?

_____

_____

_____

_____

_____

_____

_____

_____

_____

6. What does Paul call us to remember when we consider the actions and behaviors of those outside the church? How should recalling God's grace and the way that He treats us impact the way we treat others (see verses 3–8)?

_____

_____

_____

_____

_____

_____

_____

_____

_____

_____

Avoid Dissension (Titus 3:9–15)

⁹ But avoid foolish disputes, genealogies, contentions, and strivings about the law; for they are unprofitable and useless. ¹⁰ Reject a divisive man after the first and second admonition, ¹¹ knowing that such a person is warped and sinning, being self-condemned.

¹² When I send Artemas to you, or Tychicus, be diligent to come to me at Nicopolis, for I have decided to spend the winter there. ¹³ Send Zenas the lawyer and Apollos on their journey with haste, that they may lack nothing. ¹⁴ And let our people also learn to maintain good works, to meet urgent needs, that they may not be unfruitful.

¹⁵ All who are with me greet you. Greet those who love us in the faith.

Grace be with you all. Amen.

7. Paul closes his letter to Titus by mirroring his opening words of warning (see 1:10–16; see also 2 Timothy 2:23–26). Why did Paul want

Titus to avoid "disputes, genealogies, contentions, and strivings about the law" in his interactions with others (see verses 9–11)?

_____

_____

_____

_____

_____

8. Paul was a free man when he wrote this letter to Titus, but we know from his correspondence with Timothy that he would soon be imprisoned once again. Already he was feeling the rejection of those close to him. How do Paul's final instructions reveal that he valued his faithful community of friends (see verses 12–15)?

_____

_____

_____

_____

_____

REVIEWING THE STORY

Paul helps Titus recognize the potential of believers who are motivated by God's grace. He lists the qualities and attitudes that should mark the behavior of all believers—male and female, young and old, slave and free—as well as the things believers should avoid. He helps Titus understand that godly behavior not only brings glory to the Lord but also disarms the enemies of Christ. Paul emphasizes that God's grace is available to _all_, and it has real power to change lives. Our memories of the people we were before we encountered God's grace should thus serve as our motivation to live according to God's Word.

9. What happens when sound doctrine is presented with integrity, reverence, and incorruptibility (see Titus 2:6–8)?

_____

_____

_____

_____

_____

10. What did Paul say to embolden Titus in his ministry when it came to sharing the truth about God's saving grace (see Titus 2:15)?

_____

_____

_____

_____

11. What faithful saying did Paul want Titus to affirm to his congregation (see Titus 3:8)?

_____

_____

_____

_____

12. What did Paul advise Titus to do with troublemakers who refused to heed his warnings (see Titus 3:10–11)?

_____

_____

_____

_____

_____

APPLYING THE MESSAGE

13. How has God's love, kindness, and generosity been lavished on you?

_____

_____

_____

_____

_____

_____

_____

14. What are some strategies you have developed for avoiding "foolish disputes" with others?

_____

_____

_____

_____

_____

_____

_____

REFLECTING ON THE MEANING

In this final section of Paul's letter to Titus, he refers to the grace of God as our "teacher" (see 2:11). He then goes on to discuss four "subjects" in which we, as believers in Christ, can receive God's instruction as we consider His grace.

First, *grace teaches us to renounce our sin.* Paul writes that grace should lead us to "[deny] ungodliness and worldly lusts" (verse 12). When we are saved, God puts a desire within us to live differently from the way we used to live.

Second, *grace teaches us to allow the Holy Spirit to direct our lives.* Paul states, "We should live soberly, righteously, and godly in the present age" (verse 12). To "live soberly" means to think clearly and carefully about things, to have a disciplined mind, and to see things as they really are. We allow the Holy Spirit to nurture this type of "sober living" within us and are open to Him convicting us of things we might have been comfortable with before.

Third, *grace teaches us to respect others.* Paul notes that when grace rules our lives, we are "subject to rules and authorities," "speak evil of no one," and are "peaceable, gentle, showing all humility to all men" (3:1–2). Our relationships with one another as God's children—and the respect we show one another—mirrors our relationship with Christ. We take Jesus' words to heart when He said, "Assuredly, I say to you, inasmuch as you did [good works] to one of the least of these My brethren, you did it to Me" (Matthew 25:40).

Fourth, *grace teaches us to live godly lives and to resist laziness.* Paul states, "This is a faithful saying, and these things I want you to affirm constantly, that those who have believed in God should be careful to maintain good works" (Titus 3:8). We cannot be godly without God's Word, but godliness is also attained by practicing good spiritual disciplines. Again, Paul is clear that we are not saved *by* good works, but we are saved *for* good works.

God desires for us to make godly living a priority. As Paul said to the Ephesians, "For by grace you have been saved through faith, and that not of yourselves; it is the gift of God, not of works, lest anyone should boast" (Ephesians 2:8–9). Many of us stop there. But the next verse is just as essential to our spiritual well-being: "For we are His workmanship, created in Christ Jesus for good works, which God prepared beforehand that we should walk in them" (verse 10). Grace teaches us that if we have been saved, we will desire to serve God zealously.

JOURNALING YOUR RESPONSE

What impact have you seen God's gift of grace have on your life?

LEADER'S GUIDE

Thank you for choosing to lead your group through this study from Dr. David Jeremiah on *The Letters of 1 & 2 Timothy and Titus*. Being a group leader has its own rewards, and it is our prayer that your walk with the Lord will deepen through this experience. During the twelve lessons in this study, you and your group will read selected passages from these letters, explore key themes in them based on teachings from Dr. Jeremiah, and review questions that will encourage group discussion. There are multiple components in this section that can help you structure your lessons and discussion time, so please be sure to read and consider each one.

BEFORE YOU BEGIN

Before your first meeting, make sure that you and your group are well-versed with the content of the lesson. Group members should have their own copy of *The Letters of 1 & 2 Timothy and Titus study guide* prior to the first meeting so they can follow along and record their answers, thoughts, and insights. After the first week, you may wish to assign the study guide lesson as homework prior to the group meeting and then use the meeting time to discuss the content in the lesson.

To ensure everyone has a chance to participate in the discussion, the ideal size for a group is around eight to ten people. If there are more than ten people, break up the bigger group into smaller subgroups. Make sure the members are committed to participating each week, as this will help create stability and help you better prepare the structure of the meeting.

At the beginning of each week's study, start with the opening Getting Started question to introduce the topic you will be discussing. The members should answer briefly, as the goal is just for them to have an idea of the subject in their minds as you go over the lesson. This will allow the members to become engaged and ready to interact with the rest of the group.

After reviewing the lesson, try to initiate a free-flowing discussion. Invite group members to bring questions and insights they may have discovered to the next meeting, especially if they were unsure of the meaning of some parts of the lesson. Be prepared to discuss how biblical truth applies to the world we live in today.

WEEKLY PREPARATION

As the group leader, here are a few things that you can do to prepare for each meeting:

- *Be thoroughly familiar with the material in the lesson*. Make sure that you understand the content of each lesson so you know how to structure the group time and are prepared to lead the group discussion.

- *Decide, ahead of time, which questions you want to discuss*. Depending on how much time you have each week, you may not be able to reflect on every question. Select specific questions that you feel will evoke the best discussion.

- *Take prayer requests*. At the end of your discussion, take prayer requests from your group members and then pray for one another.

STRUCTURING THE DISCUSSION TIME

There are several ways to structure the duration of the study. You can choose to cover each lesson individually, for a total of twelve weeks of group meetings, or you can combine two lessons together per week, for a total of six weeks of group meetings. The following charts illustrate these options:

TWELVE-WEEK FORMAT

Week	Lessons Covered	Reading
1	Fight the Good Fight	*1 Timothy 1:1–20*
2	A Witness to the World	*1 Timothy 2:1–15*
3	Traits of a Godly Leader	*1 Timothy 3:1–16*
4	A Spiritual Workout	*1 Timothy 4:1–16*
5	Honor in the Church	*1 Timothy 5:1–25*
6	Godliness and Contentment	*1 Timothy 6:1–21*
7	Rekindle Your Faith	*2 Timothy 1:1–18*
8	Soldiers for Christ	*2 Timothy 2:1–26*
9	A Life Worthy of Imitation	*2 Timothy 3:1–17*
10	Awaiting the Crown	*2 Timothy 4:1–22*
11	God's Plan	*Titus 1:1–16*
12	God's Amazing Grace	*Titus 2:1–3:15*

SIX-WEEK FORMAT

Week	Lessons Covered	Reading
1	Fight the Good Fight / A Witness to the World	*1 Timothy 1:1–2:15*
2	Traits of a Godly Leader / A Spiritual Workout	*1 Timothy 3:1–4:16*
3	Honor in the Church / Godliness and Contentment	*1 Timothy 5:1–6:21*
4	Rekindle Your Faith / Soldiers for Christ	*2 Timothy 1:1–2:26*
5	A Life Worthy of Imitation / Awaiting the Crown	*2 Timothy 3:1–4:22*
6	God's Plan / God's Amazing Grace	*Titus 1:1–3:15*

In regard to organizing your time when planning your group Bible study, the following two schedules, for sixty minutes and ninety minutes, can give you a structure for the lesson:

Section	60 Minutes	90 Minutes
Welcome: Members arrive and get settled	5 minutes	10 minutes
Getting Started Question: Prepares the group for interacting with one another	10 minutes	10 minutes
Message: Review the lesson	15 minutes	25 minutes
Discussion: Discuss questions in the lesson	25 minutes	35 minutes
Review and Prayer: Review the key points of the lesson and have a closing time of prayer	5 minutes	10 minutes

As the group leader, it is up to you to keep track of the time and keep things moving according to your schedule. If your group is having a good discussion, don't feel the need to stop and move on to the next question. Remember, the purpose is to pull together ideas and share unique insights on the lesson. Encourage everyone to participate, but don't be concerned if certain group members are more quiet. They may just be internally reflecting on the questions and need time to process their ideas before they can share them.

GROUP DYNAMICS

Leading a group study can be a rewarding experience for you and your group members—but that doesn't mean there won't be challenges. Certain members may feel uncomfortable discussing topics that they consider very personal and might be afraid of being called on. Some members might have disagreements on specific issues. To help prevent these scenarios, consider the following ground rules:

- If someone has a question that may seem off topic, suggest that it be discussed at another time, or ask the group if they are okay with addressing that topic.

- If someone asks a question you don't know the answer to, confess that you don't know and move on. If you feel comfortable, invite other group members to give their opinions or share their comments based on personal experience.
- If you feel like a couple of people are talking much more than others, direct questions to people who may not have shared yet. You could even ask the more dominating members to help draw out the quiet ones.
- When there is a disagreement, encourage the group members to process the matter in love. Invite members from opposing sides to evaluate their opinions and consider the ideas of the other members. Lead the group through Scripture that addresses the topic, and look for common ground.

When issues arise, encourage your group to think of Scripture: "Love one another" (John 13:34), "If it is possible, as much as it depends on you, live peaceably with all men" (Romans 12:18), and, "Be swift to hear, slow to speak, slow to wrath" (James 1:19).

ABOUT
Dr. David Jeremiah and Turning Point

Dr. David Jeremiah is the founder of Turning Point, a ministry committed to providing Christians with sound Bible teaching relevant to today's changing times through radio and television broadcasts, audio series, books, and live events. Dr. Jeremiah's teaching on topics such as family, prayer, worship, angels, and biblical prophecy forms the foundation of Turning Point.

David and his wife, Donna, reside in El Cajon, California, where he serves as the senior pastor of Shadow Mountain Community Church. David and Donna have four children and twelve grandchildren.

In 1982, Dr. Jeremiah brought the same solid teaching to San Diego television that he shares weekly with his congregation. Shortly thereafter, Turning Point expanded its ministry to radio. Dr. Jeremiah's inspiring messages can now be heard worldwide on radio, television, and the internet.

Because Dr. Jeremiah desires to know his listening audience, he travels nationwide holding ministry rallies and spiritual enrichment conferences that touch the hearts and lives of many people. According to Dr. Jeremiah, "At some point in time, everyone reaches a turning point; and for every person, that moment is unique, an experience to hold onto forever. There's so much changing in today's world that sometimes it's difficult to choose the right path. Turning Point offers people an understanding of God's Word and seeks to make a difference in their lives."

Dr. Jeremiah has authored numerous books, including *Escape the Coming Night* (Revelation), *The Handwriting on the Wall* (Daniel), *Overcoming Loneliness, Prayer—The Great Adventure, God in You* (Holy

Spirit), *When Your World Falls Apart, Slaying the Giants in Your Life, My Heart's Desire, Hope for Today, Captured by Grace, Signs of Life, What in the World Is Going On?, The Coming Economic Armageddon, I Never Thought I'd See the Day!, God Loves You: He Always Has—He Always Will, Agents of the Apocalypse, Agents of Babylon, Revealing the Mysteries of Heaven, People Are Asking . . . Is This the End?, A Life Beyond Amazing, Overcomer, The Book of Signs,* and *Everything You Need.*

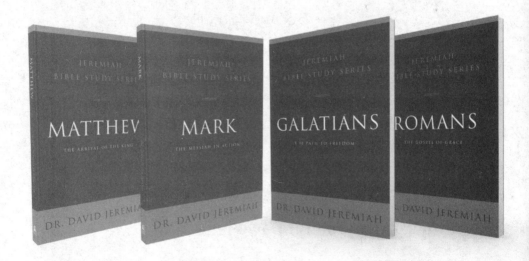